YOUNG MATHEMATICIANS
AT WORK

YOUNG MATHEMATICIANS
AT WORK

CONSTRUCTING MULTIPLICATION
AND DIVISION

CATHERINE TWOMEY FOSNOT
MAARTEN DOLK

HEINEMANN • Portsmouth, NH

Heinemann
A division of Reed Elsevier Inc.
361 Hanover Street
Portsmouth, NH, 03801-3912
www.heinemann.com

Offices and agents throughout the world

Figures 3.2, 3.3, 3.4, and 3.5 are from *Interactieve video on de nascholing rekenenwiskunde (Interactive Video for Inservice in Mathematics Education)* by F. van Galen, M. Dolk, E. Feijs, V. Jonker, N. Ruesink, and W. Uittenbogaard (1991). Produced by Universiteit Utrecht CD-ß press, Utrecht, The Netherlands. Used by permission of the Freudenthal Institute.

The photo of the tapestry "L'artithmetique" is used courtesy of the Musée national du Moyen Age, Paris, Thermas at hotel de Cluny.

This material is supported in part by the National Science Foundation under Grant No. 9550080 and Grant No. 9911841. Any opinions, findings, and conclusions or recommendations expressed in this material are those of the authors and do not necessarily reflect the views of the National Science Foundation.

Library of Congress Cataloging-in-Publication Data

Fosnot, Catherine Twomey.
  Young mathematicians at work : constructing multiplication and division /
Catherine Twomey Fosnot, Maarten Dolk.
    p. cm.
  Includes bibliographical references and index.
  ISBN 0-325-00354-8 (alk. paper)
  1. Mathematics—Study and teaching (Elementary) I. Dolk, Maarten Ludovicus
Antonius Marie, 1952– II. Title.

QA135.5 .F6318 2001
372.7—dc21

                                                                2001016587

Editors: Victoria Merecki and Leigh Peake
Cover design: Darci Mehall/Aureo Design
Cover photograph: Haynes Images
Text photographs: Herbert Seignoret
Manufacturing: Louise Richardson

Printed in the United States of America on acid-free paper

05 04 03   RRD   5

To the teachers with whom we have worked
and from whom we have learned so much

CONTENTS

CHAPTER 4: CONNECTING DIVISION TO MULTIPLICATION

CHAPTER 5: DEVELOPING MATHEMATICAL MODELS

CHAPTER 6: ALGORITHMS VERSUS NUMBER SENSE

CHAPTER 7: DEVELOPING EFFICIENT COMPUTATION WITH MINILESSONS

CHAPTER 8: ASSESSMENT

CHAPTER 9: TEACHERS AS MATHEMATICIANS

ACKNOWLEDGMENTS

The two names on the cover of this book mean only that we are the ones who finally sat down at the keyboard. The ideas included here grew out of a collaboration between researchers at the Freudenthal Institute and the faculty and staff of Mathematics in the City, a professional development program sponsored by the City College of New York. Together, we worked, reflected, talked, and experimented.

First and foremost, we thank our Dutch colleague Willem Uittenbogaard, whose voice is evident on every page. He has been an integral force in developing the project, designing and structuring the activities we use, and participating in our classroom investigations. He spent two years living and working in New York City, coteaching the institutes and follow-up courses and supporting teachers in their classrooms as they reformed their practice. We all grew to love him and respect his knowledge of mathematics, his understanding of Freudenthal's work, and his sensitivity to the cultures that are a part of New York City. The minilessons built around problem strings (see Chapter 7) are largely the result of the work he did with us. He worked tirelessly to make the program a success, and we are extremely grateful for his professionalism, his generosity, and his dedication.

Staff members Sherrin Hersch, Betina Zolkower, Emily Dann, and Judit Kerekes all made invaluable contributions as they helped teach courses and worked alongside our teachers in their classrooms. Sherrin was also the co–principal investigator on the project, registering some 450 teachers in various and sundry courses, dealing with the paperwork, and acting as our liaison with the schools. This was often thankless, time-consuming work, and we want to acknowledge the hours she gave to it, as well as the gift of her calmness and sanity. We are especially grateful for Betina's energy and intellect, for the way she challenged us to avoid trivialized word problems, pushing us instead to make the contexts rich and challenging. She was the advisor for many of the projects teachers tried in their classrooms. We thank Emily for the depth of mathematical knowledge she contributed and for commuting from Rutgers so tirelessly, always lending a supportive ear to our teachers and helping them in any way she could. We thank Judit for the many hours she donated without pay because she believed in the project.

The project's smooth operation we owe to Herbert Seignoret. Hired initially as a part-time graduate assistant, he soon began working full time, helping with budgets, payroll, data collection, and general office management. We all grew to rely on him and his amazing ability to do twenty things at once—and well.

In the fall of 2000 Toni Cameron, one of the original participants in the program, became co–principal investigator. She took on the major responsibility for the coordinating and lead teaching of our inservice offerings. Her tireless efforts doubled our enrollment. We are extremely grateful for her wonderful energy and her willingness to teach in Cathy's stead as we completed this manuscript.

We are especially grateful to the teachers and children whose voices fill these pages. The book exists because of them and the things they tried in their classrooms. The teachers saved and shared their students' work, allowed us to videotape them in the classroom, and willingly read portions of the manuscript and offered suggestions.

Many other colleagues read portions of the three volumes in this series and provided helpful comments. In the spring of 2000, Cathy spent her sabbatical at the Freudenthal Institute. While there she shared an office with Koeno Gravemeijer. He challenged us with what he has written about models, and the books are better because of his insights. Cathy's conversations with Ed de Moor, Frans van Galen, Jean Marie Kraemer, Anne Coos Vuurmans, and Arthur Bakker helped us formulate the way we describe number relations. We particularly wish to thank Marja van den Heuvel-Panhuizen, who helped us design our approach to assessment and whose work is described throughout Chapter 8.

Funding for the project came from the National Science Foundation, the New York City Public Schools, and the Exxon-Mobil Educational Foundation. We are grateful for their support. Project Construct, in Missouri, funded our work in several schools in that state, and some of the lesson transcripts are from those classrooms.

Last, we thank our editors at Heinemann, Leigh Peake, Victoria Merecki, and Alan Huisman, for their belief in the project and their insightful suggestions for tightening the manuscript.

PREFACE

This book is the second volume in a series of three. The first volume, *Young Mathematicians at Work: Constructing Number Sense, Addition, and Subtraction*, focuses on developing numeracy in young children between the ages of four and seven. This volume focuses on developing an understanding of multiplication and division in children between the ages of seven and ten.

The series is a culmination of a long and fruitful journey characterized by collaboration, experimentation, reflection, and growth. More than ten years ago we learned of each other's work with teachers in our respective countries—Cathy in the United States, Maarten in the Netherlands. Each of us cared deeply about helping mathematics teachers base their practice on how people learn mathematics, how they come to see the world through a mathematical lens—how they come to *mathematize* their world. Each of us had done research on teachers' beliefs, their vision of practice, and how these beliefs affected their decisions, and was attempting to develop inservice programs that would enable teachers to reform their practice.

Cathy had previously been involved with the SummerMath for Teachers program at Mount Holyoke College, coteaching the summer institutes and working alongside elementary teachers in their classrooms. She had also developed and directed the Center for Constructivist Teaching, a graduate preservice program at Connecticut State University. Whether she was teaching children mathematics or helping teachers learn to teach mathematics, the learning psychology commonly known as constructivism was at the core of her work.

Maarten, a researcher at the Freudenthal Institute in the Netherlands, had already helped develop inservice materials and multimedia environments for teachers. He had also directed the PANAMA inservice project in the Netherlands and helped implement the Realistic Mathematics curricula for which the Freudenthal Institute is now so widely known. Whether he was thinking about teaching children mathematics or helping teachers learn to teach mathematics, the didactic now commonly known as realistic mathematics was at the core of his work.

In the United States, much reform was already under way, aligned with the new principles and standards published by the National Council of Teachers of Mathematics. Much attention was being paid to how students learn mathematics and to what the constructivist theory of learning might mean for teaching. Teachers were encouraged to become facilitators and questioners instead of transmitters, to use manipulatives, and to foster collaborative learning and discussion in order to support learners' constructions. Although teachers began to have a good idea about how their role needed to shift, they were given little assistance in determining content and little direction regarding what problems or investigations to pursue over time.

The focus in the United States was on how to develop learners' strategies and the big ideas surrounding them. And this was important. But the sequence of activities in the curricula being developed, even when supposedly aligned with the reform, was often based on the *discipline* of mathematics. For example, fractions were taught by way of simple part-to-whole shading activities in the lower grades, then in the higher grades as ratios, as partitioning, and finally as operators. Learners' methods of developing ideas and strategies were usually discussed in relation to pedagogy (principles of learning and teacher behavior that supports learning), if at all. Constructivist-based professional development helped teachers see the big ideas their learners were struggling with, but little attention was paid to *didactics*—a scientific theory of instruction relating to developing, stretching, and supporting mathematical learning over time. (In fact, the word *didactics* often has a negative connotation in the United States, one associated with self-correcting materials and direct instruction, not with development.)

In Europe the term *didactics* has a very different meaning. The French, for example, speak of situational *didactique,* meaning problems or situations that will enable learners to grow mathematically. The Dutch structure problem contexts in order to challenge and support learners developmentally. They spend years researching the effect of a sequence of carefully crafted problems. So, too, in Japan. Together, educators mold and craft problems in ways that strengthen their power to develop mathematical thinking. Teachers try these problems and then discuss which ones worked, which ones didn't, how they might be changed, what should come next.

The didactic in the Netherlands was based primarily on the work of the renowned mathematician Hans Freudenthal. As early as the sixties, Freudenthal had argued that people learn mathematics by actively investigating realistic problems. He claimed that mathematics was actually an activity of "mathematizing" the world, of modeling, of schematizing, of structuring one's world mathematically. Working with Dutch educators for over twenty years prior to his death in 1990, he was instrumental in reforming Dutch mathematics teaching based on "realistic mathematics." Within this framework, researchers formulated "learning lines" by studying the development of mathematical ideas historically, as well as the developmental progression of children's strategies and ideas about various mathematical topics. Then they crafted a series of contexts they thought might support children's natural development, often molding problems to facilitate disequilibrium or bring insights to the fore. Finally they tested these problems with children, revised them as necessary, and prepared them as curricula. Little attention was given to pedagogy or to cognitive psychology. While children were understood to move at their own pace developmentally, the class was taught as a whole. There was little attempt to support individual investigation or inquiry or to look at the belief systems of teachers regarding learning.

The American and Dutch educators both held an important piece of the puzzle. The Americans were thinking deeply about learning; how learners needed to engage in cognitive reordering; the importance of disequilibrium, reflection, and discussion; and the importance of big ideas. Teachers were analyzing their beliefs about learning and about their pedagogy. Classrooms were taking on the flavor of active workshops. But the Americans didn't know how to support development over time, how to use context as a didactic. The Dutch did.

In the late eighties we began to collaborate seriously. Cathy brought groups of teachers from Connecticut to the Netherlands for one-week intensive workshops, organized by Maarten and his colleague Willem Uittenbogaard. Maarten and other colleagues from the Freudenthal Institute (Jan De Lange, Frans van Galen) came to Connecticut State University. In 1993, Cathy left Connecticut State University and took a position at the City College of the City University of New York. We began to design a large-scale inservice program that would involve five school districts in New York City over five years, a project known as Mathematics in the City. The project was funded by the National Science Foundation and the Exxon Educational Foundation and began in 1995.

During the next five years we worked with over 450 elementary teachers in New York City and developed several demonstration sites. Our inservice program began with a two-week intensive institute focused on teaching and learning. In this beginning institute, we attempted to deepen teachers' knowledge of the mathematics they teach and to help them see themselves as mathematicians willing to raise questions, puzzle, and mathematize. Staff members then joined these teachers in their classrooms for a year, coteaching with them as they attempted to reform their mathematics teaching. At the same time, participants took a course focused on children's strategies, the big ideas they grapple with, and the models they develop as they attempt to mathematize their world.

Throughout the project, we interviewed teachers, analyzed children's work, and videotaped lessons; together we constructed what we came to call a "landscape of learning." Classroom teachers continued to receive support as they collaborated with colleagues, and several went on to do field research and adjunct teaching with the program.

While our inservice project was successful, this series is not about the program per se. Throughout our five-year collaboration, we formulated new beliefs about learning and teaching mathematics. We challenged each other to go beyond our beginnings—to take our strengths to the table but to stay open and learn from each other. Together with our staff and our teachers, we entered new frontiers. This series offers stories from our classrooms and describes the ways we approach teaching and the contexts we use to promote investigations and inquiry. The first book in the series focuses on how very young children construct their understanding of the number system, addition, and subtraction. This volume focuses on constructing an understanding of multiplication and division in grades 3 through 5. The third book focuses on constructing an understanding of fractions, decimals, and percents in grades 5 through 8. Related inservice materials will include CD-ROMs and videotapes with accompanying manuals. Our beliefs about teaching and learning mathematics are woven throughout.

ABOUT THIS BOOK

Chapter 1 describes and illustrates our beliefs about what it means to do and learn mathematics. We discuss it as *mathematizing,* but we ground it in the progression of strategies, the development of big ideas, and the emergence of modeling because we hold a constructivist view of learning.

Chapter 2 explains what we mean by the "landscape of learning." For teachers to open up their teaching, they need to have a deep understanding of this landscape, of the strategies, big ideas, and models children construct, of the landmarks they pass as they journey toward numeracy. They also need to integrate the use of context into constructivist psychology; therefore, this chapter contrasts "word problems" with true problematic situations that support and enhance investigation and inquiry. If young learners are truly to mathematize their world, classrooms must become communities of discourse. Teachers must learn to "lead from behind." Children need to take risks, learn to investigate, be willing to analyze errors and insufficient strategies. They must be able to represent, communicate, defend, and support their strategies and solutions with mathematical arguments. Chapter 2 also provides strategies to help teachers turn their classroom into this kind of math workshop.

Chapter 3 begins our exploration of how an understanding of the concept of multiplication is developed. It describes several investigations that illustrate ways to engage and support children as they construct the important strategies and big ideas related to this topic.

Chapter 4 focuses on the strategies and big ideas related to division. Again, it describes several investigations, including transcripts of children's conversations and samples of their work.

It is impossible to talk about mathematizing without talking about modeling. Chapter 5 defines what we mean by modeling and gives examples of how learners construct models as they try to make sense of their world mathematically. In this chapter, we also describe the importance of context in developing children's ability to model and show how teachers can help children make the leap from *models of situations* to *models as tools for thinking.*

Chapters 6 and 7 focus primarily on computation. We discuss what it means to calculate using number sense and whether or not algorithms are still the goal of computation instruction. Although children must be allowed to construct their own strategies, we offer examples of minilessons that can help children go beyond their initial, often inefficient, strategies and develop a repertoire of strategies based on a deep understanding of number relations and operations. We argue for the construction of a "number space" comprising friendly numbers, neighbors, properties, and operations. We also give examples of how teachers have used strings of related problems and the open array model to develop such a "number space."

Chapter 8 deals with assessment. How does one assess mathematizing? We describe performance and portfolio assessment, but we show how they can be strengthened by making the mathematizing more visible and by using the landscape of learning as a tool. We argue that assessment should inform teaching. We also share how children in Mathematics in the City classrooms fared on standardized achievement tests.

Last, in Chapter 9, we focus on the teacher as learner. How do we help teachers begin to see themselves as mathematicians, be willing to inquire, work at their mathematical edge, appreciate puzzlement? We open a window into an inservice classroom and invite you to mathematize along with the teachers we describe.

Like all human beings, mathematicians find ways to make sense of their reality. They set up relationships, they quantify them, and they prove them to others. For teachers to engage children in this process, they must understand and appreciate the nature of mathematics themselves. They must be willing to investigate and inquire—and to derive enjoyment from doing so. The book you hold is primarily about that—how teachers and children come to see their own lived world mathematically, their journey as they pursue the hard work of constructing big ideas, strategies, and mathematical models in the collaborative community of the classroom.

YOUNG MATHEMATICIANS
AT WORK

1 | "MATHEMATICS" OR "MATHEMATIZING"?

The United States suffers from "innumeracy" in its general population, "math avoidance" among high school students, and 50 percent failure among college calculus students. Causes include starvation budgets in the schools, mental attrition by television, parents [and teachers] who don't like math. There's another, unrecognized cause of failure: misconception of the nature of mathematics. . . . It's the questions that drive mathematics. Solving problems and making up new ones is the essence of mathematical life. If mathematics is conceived apart from mathematical life, of course it seems—dead.

—Reuben Hersh

The mathematician's best work is art, a high perfect art, as daring as the most secret dreams of imagination, clear and limpid. Mathematical genius and artistic genius touch one another.

—Gösta Mittag-Leffler

It is a truism that the purpose of teaching is to help students learn. Yet in the past teaching and learning were most often seen as two separate, even polar, processes. Teaching was what teachers did. They were supposed to know their subject matter and be able to explain it well. Students were supposed to do the learning. They were expected to work hard, practice, and listen to understand. If they didn't learn, it was their fault; they had a learning disability, they needed remediation, they were preoccupied, they were lazy. Even when we spoke of development, it was usually to assess learners to see whether they were developmentally ready for the teacher's instruction.

Interestingly, in some languages, learning and teaching are the same word. In Dutch, for example, the distinction between learning and teaching is made only by the preposition. The verb is the same. Leren aan means teaching; leren van means learning. When learning and teaching are so closely related, they will be integrated in learning/teaching frameworks: teaching will be seen as closely related to learning, not only in language and thought but also in action. If learning doesn't happen, there has been no teaching. The actions of learning and teaching are inseparable.

Of course, different teachers have different styles of helping children learn. But behind these styles are frameworks based on teachers' beliefs about the learning/teaching process. These frameworks, in turn, affect how teachers interact with children, what questions they ask, what ideas they pursue, and even what activities they design or select. Teachers make many important decisions—some of them in a split second in the nitty-gritty of the classroom. In making these decisions, some teachers are led by the structure of mathematics or the textbook, others by the development of the children.

LEARNING AND TEACHING IN THE CLASSROOM

Join us in Terry Anderson's second-grade classroom in Kirkwood, Missouri. Terry has just returned from a weekend visit with her brother, who owns a candy store in Houston, Texas, and she is using the packaging of candy as a rich, real context in which her students can generate and model for themselves the mathematical ideas related to division by ten. (When children are given trivial school-type word problems, they often just ask themselves what operation is called for; the context becomes irrelevant as they manipulate numbers, applying what they know. Truly problematic contexts engage children in a way that keeps them grounded. They attempt to model the situation mathematically, as a way to make sense of it. They notice patterns, raise conjectures, and then defend them to one another.)

"When I saw my brother this weekend, he had a problem at his candy store that he wants you to help him with," Terry begins.

"Kids helping adults? Wow, that's weird!" eight-year-old Seamus responds, pride beaming in his eyes.

"My brother lives in Houston, too!" Peter exclaims. "Your brother's a lucky person owning a candy store!"

"I know." Terry's eyes twinkle. She knows she has them hooked. "And I got to go there and get free candy!"

"Free?" several children exclaim with indignation. "Why didn't you bring some back for us?"

Terry laughs. "He sells his candy in special boxes with the store's logo, a candy basket. He has to order these boxes from a special factory that prints the logo and the name of his shop, The Candy Basket, on them. His problem is that the candy is bought by weight from a different factory, and each kind comes in a separate bag. His last order had seventy-two chocolate truffles, seventy-two vanilla truffles, twenty-three chocolate-covered nuts, thirty-three chocolate-covered jelly candies, eighty chocolate-covered caramels, and sixteen chocolate-covered nougats. He wanted to make small boxes with ten assorted candies in each one, but he didn't know how many boxes he would need. I said, 'My kids and I will help you out. You send us the amounts of candies each time an order arrives and we'll figure out for you how many boxes you'll need.'"

"I've got an idea already," says Stephen, who is always quick to set to work.

"Great, Stephen. Let's all get to work with a partner and see what we come up with." Terry assigns partners, and the children get their math journals in which to record their work. "Use any materials you want, or make drawings to help you figure it out. We'll share our thinking in a math congress in about a half hour, when everyone feels he or she has had enough time to work on this."

A "math congress" is a time when the whole class gathers and children present and discuss their strategies and solutions with one another. Just as mathematicians work out formal proofs to convince their fellow mathematicians of the relationships they have been exploring, Terry's students defend and support their thinking as Terry guides their discussion to reveal important mathematical ideas and strategies. The math congress is much more than just sharing; it is a critical part of the math lesson. As children prepare to present their work, and as they think about how they will communicate their work and anticipate their classmates' questions, their own understanding deepens.

The children set to work investigating the problem. Some take out Unifix cubes; most draw and calculate. Terry moves from group to group, ensuring that everyone is busy and clear about the problem. She sits down with Elsa and Jan for a moment.

"We're trying to add up all the candies," the girls explain. "We're counting by tens. Here's seventy [*they point to a 72*] and here's twenty [*they point to the 23*]. And all that together is ninety. We had to do eighteen tens [*adding 10 (from the 16) and 80 next*], and that was 190, and we kept going and then we added on the ones. We got 396."

Terry sees that their total is off by a hundred: because they are as yet unaware of the implicit place value in the numbers, keeping track of the amounts is very difficult. However, rather than focusing on their answer, Terry wants to keep them grounded in the context as she explores their strategy. "And so what is this 396? Boxes or candies?" she asks.

Both girls look a little perplexed. Elsa says, "Boxes." Jan says, "Candies." They look at each other and laugh. Jan tries to change Elsa's thinking: "One bag has seventy-two candies. . . ."

Elsa is quick to see her error. "Oh yeah, it's candies."

"So then what is your next step?" Terry wonders.

"Figure out how many boxes he needs?" Jan asks quizzically.

"Yes, because my brother Steve needs to place the box order. How many boxes do you think he will need for 396 candies?"

"Oh. . . ." Jan pauses, thinking out loud. "Ten candies in each box. . . ." She gets an idea. "I know. We can divide these all up, ten to a box."

Elsa begins to get excited. "Oh, yeah!"

"How many tens in three hundred, though?" Jan says, rolling her eyes.

Elsa acknowledges the difficulty. "Oh . . . oh . . . a lot!"

They both laugh.

Really doing mathematics involves working at the edge of your mathematical knowledge and enjoying the puzzlement. Too often teachers try to simplify problems so that the students can more easily arrive at the teacher's answer. Little genuine puzzlement is engendered, and children never learn to value the challenge of "cracking" a problem. Terry wants her students to find ways to simplify problems themselves. She wants them to own the solutions and enjoy the process of arriving at them.

Terry nods in empathetic agreement: "This is hard. What could we do?"

"Hmm," Elsa ponders, and then seems to have an idea. "Oh, wait a minute," she exclaims.

"What did you think of?" Terry prompts.

"I thought of how many tens in a hundred," Elsa offers.

"Oh, now there's a way to start!" Terry encourages her enthusiastically.

Jan picks up on Elsa's idea and jumps in: "Yeah, and then we could do ninety!"

Both girls stand up in excitement.

"Oh, oh . . . there are thirty tens in a hundred, no . . . ten tens in a hundred . . . so thirty tens in three hundred!" Elsa reasons aloud, delighted with herself.

Terry shares their excitement and encourages them to record their thinking. "Oh, wow, do you think you should write that down before you forget it?"

"Yeah!" Elsa laughs and writes, "30 boxes for 300." "And then there's nine tens in ninety!" She writes, "9 boxes for 90," and exclaims, "I'm seeing something here!" She points out the place value pattern to Jan.

Jan sees the pattern too and turns to Terry, laughing with excitement. "We're digging deep!"

Terry laughs too, acknowledging the dramatic flair with which they are resolving their challenge. "Yes, you're digging deep!"

The girls notice that the pattern is holding. "And now we have to add these nine to thirty. Look, thirty-nine boxes for three hundred and ninety candies," they conclude.

Jan and Elsa are constructing the big idea of place value underlying division by ten. By focusing not on their answer but on their thinking, Terry has allowed them to continue exploring. Ideas like division by ten are difficult for children because of the *unitizing* involved—the understanding that ten ones are also one ten. The girls began adding up the total amount of candies by thinking about 72 as 70 plus 2, not 7 tens plus 2. Only by continuing to struggle with the problem and noticing patterns along the way did they begin to construct the idea of unitizing. Ideas like these require logico-mathematical thinking (Kamii 1985); they cannot just be explained or transmitted. Children may be able to paraphrase these ideas back if teachers explain them, but to really understand ideas like this, children must infer them on their own—and this requires setting up relationships, generalizing, and understanding why the pattern happens.

Social knowledge—how we symbolize division on paper, for example —can be transmitted or told. The symbols for division are arbitrary signifiers that mathematicians have agreed to use to represent the operation. Because Elsa and Jan have now constructed the ideas, Terry now shows them how they can represent their work with appropriate mathematical symbols.

"Here's how mathematicians would write what you did," Terry explains. She writes it three ways: $396/10$; $396 \div 10$; $10\overline{)396}$. "They all mean the same thing." Seeing the 396 written allows the girls to extend the pattern they have noticed.

"And look," Elsa exclaims, "if you take the six off, you have the answer!"

"So why don't you take a big piece of chart paper and write your pattern down, what you noticed, so that you can share it during our math congress."

What Is Revealed

This glimpse into Terry's classroom reveals a very different approach to mathematics from the one most of us experienced in our past schooling. Traditionally mathematics has been perceived as a ready-made discipline to be handed down by a teacher skilled in the art of transmitting, or explaining, clearly. In the classrooms most of us have attended, teachers stood at the chalkboard and explained place value and how to divide, many of them using only the symbols and words. They demonstrated long division procedures, and students then practiced them over and over. Some teachers may have used base ten blocks or bundled straws to explain how ten objects become one grouping of ten and how and why the long division procedures work. But the premise was always the same. The teacher was the fountain of wisdom who understood that mathematics was a discipline thought to comprise facts, concepts, formulae, and algorithms, and this discipline could be transmitted, explained, practiced, and learned if teachers were well versed in it and learners were diligent. Most students in mathematics classrooms did not see mathematics as creative but instead as something to be explained by their teacher, then practiced and applied. One might call this traditional approach "school mathematics."

Mathematicians, on the other hand, engage in quite a different practice. They make meaning in their world by setting up quantifiable and spatial relationships, by noticing patterns and transformations, by proving them as generalizations, and by searching for elegant solutions. They construct new mathematics to solve real problems or to explain or prove interesting patterns, relationships, or puzzles in mathematics itself. The renowned mathematician David Hilbert once commented that he liked to prove things in at least three or four different ways, because by doing so he better understood the relationships involved. At the heart of mathematics is the process of setting up relationships and trying to prove these relationships mathematically in order to communicate them to others. Creativity is at the core of what mathematicians do.

Interestingly, the sculptor Henry Moore described his work in much the same way Hilbert did. He said that before he sculpted something, he always drew the figure several times to learn more about it. In fact, we all find ways to make meaning from our interactions in the world. The process of constructing meaning *is* the process of learning. We create our knowledge; we do not discover it. Writers make meaning when they formulate stories and narratives, when they construct characters and plots, when they play with words and metaphors. Scientists make meaning by wondering about scientific phenomena; by hypothesizing, designing, and performing experiments; and then by proposing explanations that fit their results. Musicians hear cadence, rhythm, harmony, discordance, and melody as they interact in their world. Artists see color, form, texture, and line.

In fields other than mathematics, we've understood this constructive nature of learning. We teach students to become good writers by involving them in the process of writing. In science, we engage learners in actively inquiring, in formulating hypotheses, and in designing experiments. We teach art and music by allowing learners to create their own "masterpieces." Have we traditionally been teaching mathematics in our classrooms, or only the "history" of mathematics—some past mathematicians' constructions and their applications? Is there any connection at all between "school mathematics" and "real mathematics"?

The vignette from Terry's classroom is evidence of a different view of mathematics—one more closely akin to the process of constructing meaning—that might better be termed "mathematizing." Children are organizing information into charts and tables, noticing and exploring patterns, putting forth explanations and conjectures, and trying to convince one another of their thinking—all processes that beg a verb form. This view of mathematics was put forth by the well-known twentieth-century Dutch mathematician Hans Freudenthal (1968) when he argued that mathematics was a human activity—the process of modeling reality with the use of mathematical tools.

To generate such mathematizing, Terry immerses her students in an investigation grounded in context. As they examine the candy problem and develop their own strategies for dealing with it, they find ways to simplify the numbers by pulling them apart. They notice patterns. Then they explore these patterns and try to figure out why they are happening. They raise their own mathematical questions and discuss them in the mathematical community of their classroom. But is this only process? What about content? Do all the children construct the relationship between place value and division by ten? Is understanding that relationship even the goal that day for all the children?

Let's return to Terry's classroom as she continues to visit with and question her students. Four children, Sam, Tina, Katie, and Josh, are sitting on the floor with Unifix cubes spread all around. Terry joins them. "So tell me what you're doing. How are you guys thinking about this?"

"We're making the boxes," reports Tina. "It was a lot of work, so we decided to work together." The children are building stacks with five Unifix cubes in each and putting two stacks side by side to make boxes that are 2×5 arrays. Several of these are laid out in front of them.

"So how many candies have you packed so far?" Terry asks.

Sam counts by tens to show her. "Ten, twenty, thirty, forty, fifty, sixty, seventy, and there's two extras left. These are the chocolate truffles. Now we're doing the jellies."

"And you're going to make each kind? Then what?"

"Then we'll count all the boxes, and we'll know how many." For Katie, it's a fait accompli.

Terry suggests the group record the number of boxes and leftovers for each variety of chocolate on a chart before they combine all the leftovers to make more boxes. Because these children needed to "pack" the boxes with cubes and then count by tens, she hopes recording the varieties individually will help them notice the place value pattern that will appear.

Then she moves on to Seamus and Ned. These two boys had begun adding up all the candies but then decided this would take a long time. They proudly tell Terry about their new strategy and how fast it is.

"Look, here's the truffles." Ned points to his math journal, where he has written, "70 and 70." Underneath these numbers he has drawn lines and written, "7 and 7 = 14." "Each of these needs seven boxes," he states with a flourish.

"Oh . . . how did you know that?" Terry asks.

"Because seven times ten equals seventy."

"So you're disregarding the zeroes. That's fast. Do you mean the answer is right here?" Terry points to the tens column.

Ned and Seamus nod and tell Terry that altogether her brother will need 29 boxes. "Six candies are left over," they conclude.

"What should Steve do with the leftovers?" Terry asks.

"Well, he could order thirty boxes and just have six candies in one, or he could make twenty-nine full boxes and save the others for another shipment," Seamus offers.

As Terry moves from group to group, her questioning changes in relation to what the children are investigating and the ideas and strategies each child is in the process of constructing. Although the connection between place value and division by ten is an overall "horizon"—an overall goal Terry has purposely embedded in the context—each child is at a different place developmentally, and therefore the context is open enough to allow for individual exploration and divergence. Terry continues to support and encourage development as she leads the subsequent math congress.

"Katie, Tina, Sam, and Josh, please start us off."

The group members come to the front of the class with their Unifix cubes. "We packed the candies into boxes. When we were done we had two hundred and ninety candies packed into boxes, with six leftovers."

"Did you count by ones and then pack the candies into boxes?" Terry asks, prompting for clarification.

"No," Sam answers, "We counted by tens. . . ."

"Yeah, see," Tina interrupts, "seventy-two is seventy and two . . . so we built ten, twenty, thirty, forty, fifty, sixty, seventy."

Terry asks Bess and Jessie to share next. Although these girls did not use cubes, they also split the numbers into tens and ones. Terry wants to develop a connection between the two solutions.

To prepare for the congress, Bess and Jessie have written their work on a transparency (see Figure 1.1). They have separated out the ones-column amounts (72 becomes 70 and 2, for example) and then added each category of numbers. Bess begins their explanation: "Seventy and twenty is ninety. Then thirty more. . . ."

Terry interrupts to make sure everyone understands. "Does everyone see where they are getting their numbers, like twenty and seventy?"

Shelley raises her hand, explains where the numbers came from, and adds, "I did it that way, too. But then I noticed that if it was seventy candies, it was seven boxes."

"Oh, yeah," several children comment with surprise.

After Bess and Jessie continue with their explanations, Terry asks Elsa and Jan to share. She does this to continue the discussion of the place value pattern. Elsa and Jan describe how they noticed that the number of boxes was always the same as the number left when the units were removed—396 produces 39 boxes with 6 candies left.

FIGURE 1.1
Bess and Jessie's Strategy

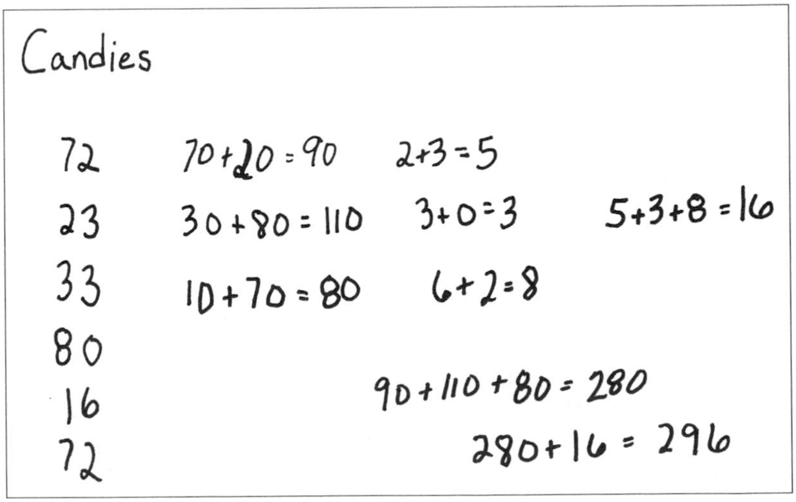

Candies

72	$70 + 20 = 90$	$2 + 3 = 5$
23	$30 + 80 = 110$	$3 + 0 = 3$ $5 + 3 + 8 = 16$
33	$10 + 70 = 80$	$6 + 2 = 8$
80		
16	$90 + 110 + 80 = 280$	
72	$280 + 16 = 296$	

"We're sure about the pattern but we need to recheck our answer," they conclude. "Just use the pattern as a shortcut," Seamus offers, describing the connection between multiplication and division: 70 divided by 10 equals 7 because 7 times 10 equals 70. So add $7 + 7 + 2 + 3 + 8 + 1$. That is 28 boxes. Sixteen more candies is one more box with 6 extras.

TEACHING AND LEARNING AS DEVELOPMENT

By varying her questioning as she monitors the congress, Terry allows her students to think further about their strategies and gives them a chance to "stretch" mathematically from wherever they are developmentally. By constructing their own strategies and defending them, all the children are immersed in an investigation that involves mathematizing. But mathematizing should not be dismissed simply as process. Mathematizing *is* content. Children are exploring ideas—unitizing, division, the connection between division and multiplication, and the place value system inherent in dividing by ten—in relation to their own level of cognitive development. As children learn to recognize, be intrigued by, and explore patterns, and as they begin to overlay and interpret experiences, contexts, and phenomena with mathematical questions, tools (such as tables and charts), and models (such as the quotative one in this problem), they are constructing what it really means to be a mathematician—to organize and interpret their world through a mathematical lens. This is the essence of mathematics.

Terry supports her children by posing questions and offering rich contexts for mathematizing. This approach enables children to take the next step in the learning process. The development of the children seems to guide Terry's teaching. But development can be nothing more than a catchword. No one would disagree that development is important. Educators have talked about developmentally appropriate practice for years. But what does development mean *in relation to mathematics learning and teaching?*

Terry's teaching reflects her appropriate understanding of development. But she does more—she employs a different framework. Her teaching is grounded in the development of *mathematical ideas*—in her knowledge of the structure of mathematics. But there is still more. She understands the paths and the horizons of the landscape of this learning; she knows how children *come to understand* different mathematical ideas. She thinks about how to employ mathematical contexts as a didactic—how to use them to facilitate mathematical learning. She knows and recognizes important landmarks along the way—strategies, big ideas, and mathematical models—and she designs her contexts with these landmarks in mind. Different contexts have the potential to generate different models, strategies, and big ideas. In Terry's framework, learning and teaching are connected. She works on the edge between the structure of mathematics and the development of the children; the value she gives one or the other differs with what happens in her classroom.

STRATEGIES, BIG IDEAS, AND MODELS IN A TEACHING/LEARNING FRAMEWORK

Strategies as Schemes

The mind is never a blank slate. Even at birth, infants have organized patterns of behavior—or schemes (Piaget 1977)—for learning and understanding the world. Beginning as reflexes (grasping and orienting, for example), these initial schemes soon become differentiated and coordinated. Children learn to crawl and then walk to objects to be grasped, felt, sucked, and explored visually. Grasping is refined to include pushing, pulling, hitting, and other forms of exploring with the fingers. Sucking is differentiated into chewing, biting, and licking. New strategies for exploration are constructed.

Children attempting to understand "how many"—how many plums there are in the grocer's box, how many stairs they have climbed after going up ten flights, how many boxes are needed to hold 296 candies—use various assimilatory schemes. They count by ones or skip count by groups. They work with familiar pieces first (how many tens in one hundred, for example). These strategies in turn evolve into efficient strategies for multiplication and division.

Developing all these strategies is no mean feat! The progression of strategies, or "progressive schematization" as Treffers (1987) calls it, is an important inherent characteristic of learning.

Big Ideas as Structures

Underlying this developmental progression of strategies is the construction of some essential big ideas. What is a "big idea" and how is it different from a strategy? Big ideas are "the central, organizing ideas of mathematics— principles that define mathematical order" (Schifter and Fosnot 1993, 35). As such, they are deeply connected to the structures of mathematics. They are, however, also characteristic of shifts in learners' reasoning—shifts in perspective, in logic, in the mathematical relationships they set up. As such, they are connected to part/whole relationships—to the structure of thought in general (Piaget 1977). In fact, that is *why* they are connected to the structures of mathematics. As mathematical ideas developed through the centuries and across cultures, the advances were often characterized by paradigmatic shifts in reasoning. These ideas are "big" because they are critical to mathematics and because they are big leaps in the development of children's reasoning.

For example, *unitizing* is one big idea we saw children grappling with in Terry's class. Unitizing underlies the understanding of place value and multiplication and division by ten; ten objects become one group of ten. Unitizing requires that children use number to count not only objects but also groups—and to count them both simultaneously. The whole is thus seen as a group of a number of objects. The parts together become the new whole, and the parts (the objects in the group) and the whole (the group) can be considered simultaneously. If we know the number of candies to be packed and how many candies are in each box, we can figure out the number of boxes needed. For learners, unitizing is a shift in perspective. Children have just learned to count ten objects, one by one. Unitizing these *ten* things as *one* thing—one group—requires them almost to negate their original idea of number. It is a huge shift in thinking for children, and in fact, was a huge shift in mathematics that took centuries to develop.

Models as Tools for Thought

Language was constructed to signify meaning. When we construct an idea, we want to communicate it: through time and across cultures humans have developed language to do so. Initially, language represents ideas and actions; it is *a representation of thought*. Eventually it serves as *a tool for thought*.

Numerals were developed to signify the meaning of counting. Operational symbols like $\times$ and $\div$ were constructed to represent the actions of iterating and portioning equivalent-sized groups. While these symbols were initially developed to represent mathematical ideas, they become tools, mental images, to think with.

To speak of mathematics as mathematizing demands that we address mathematical models and their development. To mathematize, one sees, organizes, and interprets the world through and with mathematical models. Like language, these models often begin simply as representations of situations, or problems, by learners. For example, learners may initially represent a situation with Unifix cubes or with a drawing, as the children did when they used Unifix cubes to create their 2×5 arrays. These models of situations eventually become generalized as learners explore connections between and across them.

Teachers can use models as a didactic to promote the development of informal solutions specific to a context into more formal generalizable solutions—to develop models *of* thinking into models *for* thinking (Beishuizen, Gravemeijer, and van Lieshout 1997; Gravemeijer 1999). For example, using "open arrays" to represent children's computation strategies (see Chapter 5) can enable children to develop a sense of "number space"—a mental image of number based on relationships and operations (Lorenz 1997).

Walking the Edge

Terry walks the edge between the structure of mathematics and the development of the child by considering the progression of strategies, the big ideas involved, and the emergent models. Ultimately what matters is the mathematical activity of the learner—how the learner mathematizes the situations that Terry designs. But learning—development—is complex. Strategies, big ideas, and models are all involved—they all need to be developed as they affect one another. They are the steps, the shifts, and the mental maps in the journey. They are the components in a "landscape of learning."

Strategies, big ideas, and models, however, are not static points in a landscape. They are dynamic movements on the part of a learner in a journey of mathematical development. From this perspective they need to be understood as schematizing rather than as strategies, as structuring rather than as big ideas, and as modeling rather than as models (Freudenthal 1991). Teaching needs to facilitate this development. Only then can teaching and learning be seen as interrelated—for the connected teaching/learning framework that it is. This is the framework behind Terry's decision making.

SUMMING UP . . .

Look again at the epigraphs to this chapter. "It's the questions that drive mathematics. Solving problems and making up new ones is the essence of mathematical life. If mathematics is conceived apart from mathematical life, of course it seems—dead." When mathematics is understood as mathematizing one's world—interpreting, organizing, inquiring about, and constructing meaning through a mathematical lens—it becomes creative and alive. "The mathematician's best work is art, a high perfect art, as daring as the most secret dreams of imagination, clear and limpid. Mathematical genius and artistic genius touch one another."

Traditionally mathematics has been taught in our schools as if it were a dead language. It was something that past, mostly dead, mathematicians had created—something that needed to be learned, practiced, and applied. When the definition of mathematics shifts toward "the activity of mathematizing one's *lived* world," the constructive nature of the discipline and its connection to problem solving become clear.

When we define mathematics in this way, and teach accordingly, children will rise to the challenge. They will grapple with mathematical ideas; they will develop and refine strategies as they search for elegance; they will create mathematical models as they attempt to understand and represent their world. Because this process of mathematizing is constructive, teachers need to walk the edge between the structure of mathematics and the development of the learner. This edge is a journey across a landscape of learning comprising strategies, big ideas, and models. From the perspective of mathematics as mathematizing, it is the mathematical activity of the learner that ultimately matters; thus, strategies, big ideas, and models need to be understood as schematizing, structuring, and modeling. Teaching needs to be seen as inherently connected to learning.

Children, in learning to mathematize their world, will come to see mathematics as the living discipline it is, with themselves a part of a creative, constructive mathematical community, hard at work.

2 | THE LANDSCAPE OF LEARNING

It is not knowledge but the act of learning, not possession but the act of getting there, which grants the greatest enjoyment. When I have clarified and exhausted a subject, then I turn away from it, in order to go into darkness again; the never satisfied man is so strange. . . . If he has completed a structure, then it is not in order to dwell in it peacefully, but in order to begin another. I imagine the world conqueror must feel thus, who, after one kingdom is scarcely conquered, stretches out his arms for others.

—Karl Friedrich Gauss

DESCRIBING THE JOURNEY

Linear Frameworks

Historically, curriculum designers did not use a developmental framework like Terry's when they designed texts, nor did they see mathematics as mathematizing—as activity. They employed a teaching/learning framework based on the accumulated content of the discipline. They analyzed the structure of mathematics and delineated teaching and learning objectives along a line. Small ideas and skills were assumed to accumulate eventually into concepts (Gagné 1965; Bloom, Hastings, and Madaus 1971). For example, simplistic notions of fractions were considered developmentally appropriate for early childhood if they were taught as a shaded part of a whole or with pattern blocks. Later, around third grade, the equivalence of fractions was introduced, and still later, in fifth or sixth grade, operations with fractions. Development was considered but only in relation to the content: from simple to complex skills and concepts.

Focusing only on the structure of mathematics leads to a more traditional way of teaching—one in which the teacher pushes the children toward procedures or mathematical concepts because these are the goals. In a framework like this, learning is understood to move along a line. Each lesson, each day, is geared to a different objective, a different "it." All children are expected to understand the same "it," in the same way, at the end of the lesson. They are assumed to move along the same path; if there are individual differences it is just that some children move along the path more slowly—hence, some need more time or remediation. Figure 2.1 depicts such a linear framework.

Learning Trajectories

As the reform mandated by the National Council for Teachers of Mathematics has taken hold, curriculum designers and educators have tried to develop other frameworks. Most of these approaches are based on a better understanding of children's learning and of the development of tasks that will challenge them. One important finding is that children do not all think the same way. These differences in thinking are obvious in the dialogue in Terry's classroom. Although all the children in the class worked on the candy box problem, they worked in different ways, exhibited different strategies, and acted in the environment in different mathematical ways.

Marty Simon (1995) describes a learning/teaching framework that he calls a "hypothetical learning trajectory." The learning trajectory is hypothetical because, until students are really working on a problem, we can never be sure what they will do or whether and how they will construct new interpretations, ideas, and strategies. Teachers expect their students to solve a problem in a certain way. Or, even more refined, their expectations are different for different children. Figure 2.2 depicts a hypothetical learning trajectory.

Simon uses the metaphor of a sailing voyage to explain this learning trajectory:

> You may initially plan the whole journey or only part of it. You set out sailing according to your plan. However, you must constantly adjust because of the conditions that you encounter. You continue to acquire knowledge about sailing, about the current conditions, and about the areas that you wish to visit. You change your plans with respect to the order of your destinations. You modify the length and nature of your visits as a result of interactions with people along the way. You add destinations that prior to the trip were unknown to you. The path that you travel is your [actual] trajectory. The path that you anticipate at any point is your "hypothetical trajectory." (136–37)

As this quote makes clear, teaching is a planned activity. Terry did not walk into her classroom in the morning wondering what to do. She had planned her lesson, and she knew what she expected her students to do. As the children responded, she acknowledged the differences in their thinking and in their strategies, and she adjusted her course accordingly. While she honored divergence, development, and individual differences, she also had identified landmarks along the way that grew out of her knowledge of mathematics and mathematical development. These helped her plan, question, and decide what to do next.

Over the last five years, the Mathematics in the City staff have been helping teachers like Terry develop and understand what we originally called "learning lines"—hypothetical trajectories comprising the big ideas, the mathematical models, and the strategies that children construct along the way as they grapple with key mathematical topics (number, place value, addition and subtraction, multiplication and division, and so on). In conjunction with these teachers, we analyzed children's work, we looked at videotapes of lessons, and we interviewed children. We discussed the *strategies* (and their progression—the schematizing) that children used as they acted within the environment mathematically. We attempted to specify the important *big ideas* the children grappled with for each topic. And we focused on *mathematical modeling,* whereby students see, organize, and interpret their world mathematically.

Although we still believe that knowledge of models, strategies, and big ideas will enable teachers to develop a "hypothetical learning trajectory," we have stopped calling it a learning line—the term seems too linear. Learning—real learning—is messy (Duckworth 1989). We prefer instead the metaphor of a landscape.

FIGURE 2.1
Linear Framework

FIGURE 2.2
*Hypothetical Learning
Trajectory (Simon 1995)*

The big ideas, strategies, and models are important landmarks for Terry as she journeys with her students across the landscape of learning. As she designs contexts for her students to explore, her goal is to enable them to act on, and within, the situations mathematically and to trigger discussions about them. Terry also has horizons in mind when she plans—horizons like place value or multiplication and division. As she and the children move closer to a particular horizon, landmarks shift, new ones appear.

The paths to these landmarks and horizons are not necessarily linear, and there are many such paths, not just one. As in a real landscape, the paths twist and turn; they cross one another, are often indirect. Children do not construct each of these ideas and strategies in an ordered sequence. They go off in many directions as they explore, struggle to understand, and make sense of their world mathematically. Strategies do not necessarily affect the development of big ideas, or vice versa. Often a big idea, like division by ten or unitizing, will affect counting strategies; but just as often "trying out" new counting strategies (like skip counting) they have seen others use will help students construct insightful relationships. Ultimately, what is important is how children function in a mathematical environment (Cobb 1997)—how they mathematize.

It is not up to us, as teachers, to decide which pathways our students will use. Often, to our surprise, children will use a path we have not encountered before. That challenges us to understand the child's thinking. What is important, though, is that we help all our students reach the horizon. When we drive a car down the road, our overall attention is on the horizon. But we also see the line in the middle of the road and use it to direct the car in the right direction. Once that line is behind us, however, it no longer serves that purpose. It is the same with teaching. When a child is still counting all or recounting from the beginning, the teacher designs activities to support the development of counting on or skip counting. However, when a child understands skip counting, when it seems that landmark has been passed, the teacher has already shifted the landmarks on the horizon to unitizing and using the distributive property.

When we are moving across a landscape toward a horizon, the horizon seems clear. But as we near it, new objects—new landmarks—come into view. So, too, with learning. One question seemingly answered raises others. Children seem to resolve one struggle only to grapple with another. Teachers must have the horizons in mind when they plan activities, when they interact, question, and facilitate discussions. But horizons are not fixed points in the landscape; they are constantly shifting. Figure 2.3 depicts the landscape-of-learning framework.

The learning-and-teaching landscape is a beautiful painting. But is it more metaphoric than real? If learners can take so many paths and the horizons are constantly shifting, how do teachers ever manage? How do we help each child make the journey and still keep in mind the responsibility we have for the class as a whole?

Terry chooses a context (the candy box) and structures patterns of tens within this context because she knows that unitizing—understanding that ten candies is also one group of ten and therefore one box—is a big idea. She chooses to discuss the place value pattern, which Seamus, Ned, and Shelley notice, because she knows that division by ten involves unitizing and that it is an important mathematical idea. She is aware, as she walks around the room, of the strategies children are using when they calculate—whether they count one by one or skip count or use the distributive property while multiplying. She notices because she knows these strategies are significant in the mathematical development of the children—they are representative of the ways children are schematizing, or acting, in a mathematical environment (Cobb 1997).

Word Problems vs. Truly Problematic Situations

One could argue that the use of context in mathematics teaching is not new. Certainly we all have vivid memories of word problems. Usually, however, our teachers assigned them after they had explained operations or formulae, and we were expected to apply these algorithms to the problems. In Terry's class, context is not being used for *application* at the end of a unit of instruction. It is being used at the start, for *construction*. Nor is the candy box context a trivial, camouflaged attempt to elicit "school mathematics." It is a rich, truly problematic situation that is real to the students, that allows them to generate and explore mathematical ideas, that can be entered at many levels, and that supports mathematizing.

Much reform is currently under way in schools in accordance with the new National Council for Teachers of Mathematics (NCTM) *Principles and Standards for School Mathematics* (2000), and many teachers are attempting to use problems to construct understanding rather than to teach

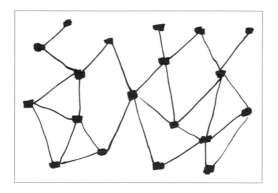

FIGURE 2.3
Landscape of Learning

by telling. But many of the problems teachers introduce are still traditional word problems. Join us in another classroom, and we'll show you what we mean.

Susan, a second-grade teacher, is reading to five children grouped around her. "'Mary went to the candy store—'" She turns to the children. "Do you want me to read it, or do you want to?"

Several of the children chorus, "You."

Susan continues. "'Mary went to the candy store to buy some candy. She bought seventy-nine pieces. If the clerk put only ten pieces in a bag, how many bags did he fill?'" She pauses, thinks about what she has read, and then although it is not part of the original problem, adds, "And how many candies were in the bag that wasn't full?"

Susan begins by involving the children in solving a problem. She is not asking them to apply an algorithm, but instead she asks them to think—to solve the problem in a way that makes sense to them. She is attempting to promote construction, not application. She is clear about the mathematics (place value and division by ten) she wants the children to explore, and she structures the context to support development, just as Terry did. But could Susan's context be stronger? Do the children become invested in the problem? Do they mathematize it?

One of the children, Michael, starts to take a handful of base ten materials out of a nearby bin, then puts them back, commenting, "Oh, I don't need these, easy." Other children comment that they are confused. One of these children, Josh, questions, "Just any bag? What do you mean . . . by a bag?"

Susan attempts to clarify the confusion. "Look at my question. 'How many bags did he fill?' And filled would mean ten candies. . . ." She pauses, then adds, "And obviously there is one bag that isn't full. I wouldn't ask the question otherwise."

This how-many-candies-in-a-bag scenario is one children can imagine (in many candy stores, candy is stored in large bins and scooped into small bags when purchased), and in that sense it is realistic. But it is not likely to promote mathematizing. It is not likely to cause children to interpret their lived world on the basis of mathematical models. It is closed, with an expected answer of "seven with nine candies left over"—a camouflaged attempt at eliciting $79/10 = 7 \text{ r } 9$. But why must there be ten candies in a bag? Candies are usually sold by weight, not quantity. And even if one accepts that ten and only ten pieces can be put in a bag, is the answer seven bags, or 7.9 bags, or eight bags with one bag short one candy? No wonder there is initial confusion when Susan reads the problem. In real life, the remainder needs to be considered and dealt with. Because the children are confused, Susan must clarify. She attempts to steer the children toward the place value pattern that she wants them to notice by adding the question, "How many candies in the bag that wasn't full?" Unfortunately, now there is almost nothing left to solve, since the children are told that one bag won't be full. The context becomes irrelevant, and the children will sacrifice their own meaning making to accommodate what Susan wants.

Two children respond, "Oh, that's easy." A third, Annie, remains confused.

Susan repeats the problem. "Think about it. Mary buys seventy-nine candies. The clerk puts ten candies in a bag. How many bags can he fill?"

Annie quickly says, "Oh, six—no, seven."

At first Susan does not acknowledge the correctness of Annie's answer, responding, "Think about it, because you'll have to tell me how you figured it out, won't you."

But Annie's confusion is still apparent. "I don't get it."

"Okay." Susan attempts to give Annie more time. "Josh is going on to think of another way to figure it out. Maybe the rest of you would like to find another way, too, while we give Annie more time to think about it."

Annie responds with more conviction, "Seven . . . because ten goes into seventy-nine."

This time Susan acknowledges Annie's thinking. "Okay, that is seven bags, so how many in the bag that isn't full?"

Susan is patient as she reminds Annie that she will have to explain her thinking. She does not supply an answer, nor does she acknowledge the correctness of Annie's first solution—that would stop her from thinking. To give Annie the time she needs, Susan encourages the other children to work on another strategy. But is the problem rich enough to benefit from exploring alternative strategies? What alternative strategies are there?

Teachers often confuse tools with strategies. Unifix cubes or base ten blocks or paper and pencil are not different strategies. They are different tools. Representing the problem with stacks of Unifix cubes grouped into tens, or with base ten blocks, or by writing 10 seven times are all the same mathematically. No benefit is derived by changing tools unless the new tool helps the child develop a higher level of schematizing (in this case, moves the child from counting by ones to employing repeated addition of tens). Is this context rich enough for that?

Susan turns to all the children and invites them to begin a discussion. "Who would like to explain how he or she figured it out? And I would like the rest of you to listen, and if you have a question, ask."

Annie offers to begin. "If there are seventy-nine candies, and if you put ten in each bag . . . [she counts the appropriate base ten rods as she continues] ten, twenty, thirty, forty, fifty, sixty, seventy, so that would be seven. How many were in the bag that wasn't full? Nine. These [she points to the unit cubes] are only nine, not ten. And each of these [she points to the rods] is a group of ten."

Susan points to the rods and acknowledges Annie's statement. "These are groups of ten." Then she turns to Michael. "Michael, you did it without cubes . . . you started to take them and then put them back. Can you explain what you did?"

"Yeah, you just take the seven from the tens and put it down. The tens are over here [*he points to the tens column*]. So I just knew seven bags. Then you take the nine from the ones. So you take the nine and put it there."

Note the language Michael uses: "take the seven from the tens," "take the nine from the ones." He treats the problem abstractly. He already knows the mathematics; the context is irrelevant. The strategies explained thus far are either counting by tens or knowing the mathematics already. Let's look at a few more responses.

"So you just knew that the seven meant seven tens?" Susan rephrases. "Any other different ways? Josh?"

Josh's strategy is similar to Annie's. He also counts by tens. "There were seventy-nine candies, and the seventy candies . . . each one of those was a ten [*he uses his fingers to demonstrate*] so . . . ten, twenty, thirty, forty, fifty, sixty, seventy. Each of those was a bag [*he holds up seven fingers*]. The nine was left over. I put it there."

Susan asks, "Did you just know that but use your fingers to prove it?" Josh acknowledges that he just knew. Susan then turns to Nora, who comments, "I just knew, too." Susan concludes the lesson with, "That's something that is really neat about our number system, remembering that the seven stands for seven tens. It makes it easy to use."

When a context is real and meaningful for children, their conversation relates to the context. They mathematize the situation. They talk about bags, boxes, and candies. They use a variety of strategies. Mathematical questions arise.

Noticing how children are thinking about a problem, noticing whether they stay grounded in the context, tells the teacher whether or not the context is a good one. When the context is a good one, the children talk about the situation. When a problem is camouflaged school mathematics, children talk about number abstractly; they lose sight of the problem as they try to figure out what the teacher wants.

Terry's context had the potential for genuine mathematizing as her students prepared charts showing the number of boxes Terry's brother would need. As the class investigated several additional candy orders, patterns appeared in the data on their tables, and these patterns triggered additional explorations. In contrast, the context in traditional word problems quickly becomes unimportant; children say "seven with nine left" or "seven tens" rather than "seven bags." And once they have an answer to the "teacher's question," they see no reason to employ alternative strategies or to inquire further.

Finding Situations for Mathematizing

If the goal of mathematics instruction is to enable children to mathematize their reality, then situations with the potential to develop the ability to mathematize need to be carefully designed (or found). To encourage children to become mathematically literate—to see themselves as mathematicians—we need to involve them in making meaning in their world mathematically. Traditionally, we have told young learners that mathematics is all around us—but we have given trivial examples, such as seeing numerals on signs, in telephone numbers, and in addresses or seeing geometric shapes in dishes, cups, boxes, and other objects in our environment.

Situations that are likely to be mathematized by learners have at least three components:

1. The potential to model the situation is built in (Freudenthal 1973). Cartons of soda six-packs, dozens of eggs, patios made of square tiles, or candy boxes all can be modeled by arrays and used to develop ideas about multiplication and division. Grocery and retail store scenarios, sharing money, collecting data and finding ways to organize them, taking inventory of materials in the classroom, all have the potential to develop mathematical modeling. Using the same model over time in different situations allows it to become generalized.

2. The situation allows children to *realize what they are doing.* It can be imaginary, or fictitious, but children are able to experience or imagine it and are able to think and act within its parameters (Fosnot and Dolk 2001). A child packing candies into boxes can picture or imagine the mathematics concretely and can check the reasonableness of answers and actions; putting ten pieces of candy into bags in a candy store makes no sense, since in this context customers pay by weight, not by number of pieces. The Dutch use the term *zich realiseren,* meaning "to realize in the sense of to picture or imagine something concretely" (van den Heuvel-Panhuizen 1996).

3. The situation prompts learners to ask questions, notice patterns, wonder, ask why and what if. Inquiry is at the heart of what it means to mathematize. Questions come from interacting with the world around us, from setting up relationships, from trying to solve problems. When the problem is "owned," it begins to come alive.

Building in Constraints

Learners' initial informal strategies are not the endpoint of instruction; they are the beginning. Teachers must transform these initial attempts into more formal and coherent mathematical strategies and models. Although peer discussions and teacher questioning can lead students to restructure their initial ideas, building constraints into the context is often a more powerful means to that end. Both Terry and Susan chose to pack candy in groups of ten because ten is an important landmark number in our number system and because division by ten in itself is an important idea. But we can also build potentially realized suggestions and constraints into contexts. For example, Betina Zolkower (1998) took a picture of a city building showing 225 windows arranged in fifteen 3 × 5 arrays (see Figure 2.4). Faced with this fragment of city life, the question "How many windows?" comes immediately to mind. As one child suggested while looking at the picture, "The windows look so worn out; maybe they will want to put in new ones, so they first need to know how many there are." Children can find the number of windows by counting by ones if they need to, but the array arrangement suggests a number of higher-level strategies: pairing two 15s to make 30, then adding 30 seven times, and finally adding one more 15; adding 15 three times, then adding 45 five times; or breaking down 15 sets of 15 windows each into 15 × 10 and 15 × 5 and then adding the two results.

The latter, more efficient, strategy, which is based on the distributive property, can be the focus during a math congress discussion, but a more powerful approach is to use other pictures with built-in constraints that re-

FIGURE 2.4
225 Windows Arranged in 3 × 5 Arrays (Zolkower 1998)

FIGURE 2.5
Soda Bottles (Zolkower 1998)

strict repeated addition or skip counting. For example, most of the four-packs of soda bottles in Figure 2.5 are obscured by the crates; this makes it hard to count by fours and implicitly suggests a minimum grouping of sixteen (the number of bottles in each crate).

Or take yet another example. Wendy Watkins, a third-grade teacher in Columbia, Missouri, told her students about a visit she made to a marina one evening. The marina had fourteen piers, each having berths for eighteen boats. She could see the berths along four piers from where she was standing. The remaining piers were obscured in the twilight. Because she hadn't been able to count all the berths individually, she asked her students whether they could come up with a way to determine how many boats the marina could hold. This scenario supports the development of the distributive property $(10 \times 18 + 4 \times 18 = 14 \times 18)$.

Open vs. Closed Situations

Real learning is constructive and developmental. As children attempt to make sense of a situation and its context, they interpret, organize, and model it based on the ideas or strategies they have already constructed. They schematize and structure it so that it makes sense. Piaget (1977) called this process *assimilation*, meaning "to make similar." The process of assimilation has often been misunderstood as *a taking in*. Rather, it is *an acting on*. We act on experiences when we attempt to understand them using strategies for interpreting, inferring, and organizing. We build new ideas on old ones, or reformulate old ideas into new ones.

Learners will assimilate contexts in many ways. In every classroom, developmental differences will affect perceptions and strategies. And any new ideas constructed will be directly linked in learners' minds to *their* past ideas, because they arise from reorganizing the initial ideas.

In Terry's class, the students employ any number of ideas, inquiries, and strategies. The goal is not the same for everyone every day, but there is equal opportunity for everyone to learn because the situations and their contexts are so open. The candy box activity offers many entry points for children, from counting the candies (as represented by Unifix cubes) one by one, to packing boxes of tens, to working with the total number of candies first, to working with the individual kinds of candy using place value. Terry varies her questions to stretch and support individual children's learning.

Closed situations have only one possible strategy. Everyone is supposed to solve the problem in the same way, and learners are either successful or unsuccessful—they either get it or they don't. Open situations, crafted so-phisticatedly with a didactical use of context, allow for and support developmental differences, and thus can facilitate mathematical development for everyone.

Word Problems vs. Context Problems

Word problems on the surface appear to offer many possible strategies by which to arrive at a solution. But because they are often designed with little context, they are usually nothing more than superficial, camouflaged attempts to get children to do the procedures teachers want them to do— procedures that have little to do with genuine mathematizing. Context problems, on the other hand, are connected as closely as possible to children's lives, rather than to "school mathematics." They are designed to anticipate and develop children's mathematical modeling of the real world. Thus, they encourage learners to invent genuine diverse solutions. In addition, context problems have built-in constraints in an attempt to support and stretch initial mathematizing. In this sense, their purpose is to promote the *development* of mathematizing. But is even this enough?

Context-based Investigations and Inquiries

If genuine mathematizing involves setting up relationships, searching for patterns, constructing models, and proposing conjectures and proving them, then context must be used in a way that simultaneously involves children in problem solving *and* problem posing. Terry could simply have asked her students to figure out how many truffles her brother would have left over after he boxed seventy-two of them. This is a real situation, one that children could mathematize in many ways because the box array contains two rows of five. They could count; they could make groups of five and skip count by fives, or count the groups; they could combine two groups of five into ten; and so on. But would children have noticed the place value pattern that Shelley noticed? Would Elsa and Jan have felt as though they were working at the edge of their knowledge ("digging deep")?

To allow the students to notice patterns, the situation and its context had to be open enough that patterns in data would appear. Piaget (1977) argued that the setting up of correspondences by learners was the beginning of the development of an understanding of relationships. Constructing a connection, a pattern, or a correspondence between objects fosters reflection. Learners begin to wonder why; they want to explain and understand the connections they notice. By asking her students to make a chart for her brother, Terry opens the situation to become a genuine investigation rather than a problem, and the children can begin to construct relationships from the patterns they notice. But still this is not enough.

Terry must also facilitate the students' questions. As they raise inquiries, Terry gets excited along with them and deliberately gets them to discuss their ideas. She supports their inquiries by giving them time and materials to pursue them. If she had not facilitated this aspect of mathematizing—the problem posing—but instead had relied on a series of context problems to be solved (even when carefully structured day by day), she would not have developed in the children the ability to mathematize *their* lived world. Some children would have been lost along the way as the class as a whole moved from activity to activity. Instead, by using context-based *investigations* and by facilitating *inquiry* in relation to them, Terry involves her children in genuine mathematizing, in being young mathematicians at work.

TURNING CLASSROOMS INTO MATHEMATICAL COMMUNITIES

Knowing the difference between word problems, context problems, investigations, and inquiries, and knowing how to keep them open, helps Terry support each child. Understanding how to mold contexts is an important didactical tool to stretch each child. But understanding the role of context is not enough. Terry also makes her classroom a community in which her students can investigate and share with one another. Developing a community that supports risk taking and mathematical discussions is another critical pedagogical component for fostering real investigations and inquiries, real mathematizing.

The Edge Between the Individual and the Community

Teaching has two important and very different phases. At home, at night, we prepare for the next day. We replay the day just past, remembering the successes, evaluating the inquiries, celebrating the insights some of the children had, recalling the stumbling blocks and the struggles—all from the perspective of mathematical development, with a sense of the landscape of learning. Although our reflections begin with individual children, as we plan we shift our attention to the community—the whole class. Our intent is to keep everyone in the community moving—to move the community as a whole across the landscape toward the horizon. No matter what path a child is on, no matter where on that path the child is, we want to move that child closer to the horizon. Fortunately, we do not need to plan separate lessons for each child—nor could we. Instead we can focus on the community, thinking of contexts and situations that will be likely to move the community as a whole closer to the horizon. To that end, our lessons must be open and rich enough that each community member can enter them and be challenged.

The next day, in class, our role changes dramatically. We become a member of the community. We listen to and interact with the children. We try to understand what each child is thinking. We decide whether to ask for clarification. We pose questions that will cause children to think. We are intrigued with individual inquiries and solutions. We think about how members of the community can help one another, how they can scaffold their ideas upon others' ideas. The night before, we are curriculum designers— designing the environment for the community. In class, we are researchers and guides. We journey with the children.

Therein lies our duality: we are community members, yet we plan for the community. We facilitate conversation around mathematical ideas and strategies for the community to consider. But, as a member of the community, we help develop the norms of what it means to prove something, of what counts as a solution, or a conjecture. We walk the edge between the community and the individual.

Facilitating Dialogue

Turning a classroom of between twenty and thirty individuals into a community is not easy: it's a structure very different from the classrooms most of us attended. Traditionally, dialogue in a classroom bounced from teacher to student, back to the teacher, then to another student. The teacher was there to question and give feedback. She stood at the front of the classroom; the learners were spread out in front of her.

In a "community of discourse" (Fosnot 1989), participants speak to one another. They ask questions of one another and comment on one another's ideas. They defend their ideas to the community, not just to the teacher. Ideas are accepted in the community insofar as they are shared and not disproved. The community develops its own norms for what it means to prove one's argument, for what stands as a mathematical problem, for how data get collected, represented, and shared. As a member of the community (but walking the edge), the teacher facilitates, monitors, and at times provides counterexamples and/or highlights connections to ensure that this dialogue supports genuine mathematical learning.

Several strategies can be helpful. After a student shares an idea, we can ask, "How many of you understand this point well enough to rephrase it in your own words?" (Or, as Terry did, "Who understands what Shelley is noticing?") The students' responses tell us not only how many of them appear to understand but also *how* they understand, how they are schematizing, structuring, and modeling. Discussion cannot happen if the community is not considering the speaker's thinking. Because construction, not transmission, lies at the heart of learning, everyone is responsible for thinking about and commenting on one another's ideas. After several children have paraphrased an idea and we are confident that most students are participating, we can ask follow-up questions: *Does anyone have a question? Who agrees? Who disagrees? Does anyone have a different idea or a different way of thinking about it?* Questions like these keep the dialogue bouncing from student to student, from community member to community member.

Investigations

When classrooms are workshops—when learners are inquiring, investigating, and constructing—there is already a feeling of community. In workshops learners talk to one another, ask one another questions, collaborate, prove and communicate their thinking to one another. The heart of math workshop is this: investigations are ongoing, and teachers try to find situations and structure contexts that will enable children to mathematize their lives—that will move the community toward the horizon. Children have the opportunity to explore, to pursue inquiries, and to model and solve problems in their own creative ways. Searching for patterns, raising questions, and constructing one's own models, ideas, and strategies are the primary focus of math workshop. The classroom becomes a community of learners engaged in activity, discourse, and reflection.

Math Congress

After investigating and writing up solutions and conjectures, the community convenes for a "math congress." This is more than just a whole-group share. The congress continues the work of helping children become mathematicians in a mathematics community. Mathematicians communicate their ideas, solutions, problems, proofs, and conjectures to one another. In fact, mathematical ideas are held as "truth" only insofar as the mathematical community accepts them as true.

In a math congress, young learners—young mathematicians at work—defend their thinking. Out of the congress come ideas and strategies that form the emerging discipline of mathematics in the classroom. The sociocultural aspects of this emerging discipline are directly connected to the community. What holds up as a proof, as a convincing argument? What counts as a beautiful idea or an efficient strategy? How will ideas be symbolized? What is mathematical language? What does it mean to talk about mathematics? What tools count as mathematical tools? What makes a good mathematical question? What serves as a conjecture? All of these questions get answered in the interactions of the community. The answers arise from the sociocultural norms and mores that develop.

Once again we as teachers are on the edge. We must walk the line between the structure and the development of mathematics, and between the individual and the community. As we facilitate discussions, as we decide which ideas to focus on, we develop the community's norms and mores with regard to mathematics, and we stretch and support individual learners. We move the community toward the horizon, *and* we enable individuals to travel their own path.

We can structure math congresses in many ways. If we want to focus on a big idea or illuminate mathematical modeling, we can bring out the connections between different solutions and strategies. If we want to refine strategies, we can scaffold the discussion from less efficient to more efficient solutions. Our goal is always to develop mathematizing—to promote shifts in thinking, to help learners develop mental maps. We focus on the community's journey, yet we work toward each student's construction of meaning.

Minilessons

A description of math workshop would not be complete without a few words about minilessons. Several minilessons are described in this book, particularly in Chapter 7. Often we may wish to highlight a computational strategy, share a problem-solving approach, or discuss what makes a valid proof. A ten-minute minilesson at the start of math workshop is a great way to do so. In a minilesson, we as teachers take a more explicit role in bringing ideas and strategies to the surface. But once again we walk the edge. We put forth ideas for the community to consider, but we must allow individuals to construct their own meaning.

SUMMING UP . . .

Learning and teaching are interrelated; one does not occur without the other. Genuine learning is not linear. It is messy, arrived at by many paths, and characterized by different-sized steps and shifts in direction. Genuine teaching is directed toward landmarks and horizons. The epigraph to this chapter quotes the great mathematician Karl Gauss: "It is not knowledge but the act of learning, not possession but the act of getting there, which grants the greatest enjoyment." As we learn, we construct. We near the horizon only to have new landmarks appear. Because learning is not linear, teaching cannot be either. If we as teachers have a deep knowledge of the landscape of learning—the big ideas, the strategies, and the models that characterize the journey—we can build contexts that develop children's ability to mathematize. By opening up situations into investigations and facilitating inquiry, we can support children's journeys along many paths.

But we need to walk the line between supporting individuals and planning for the community. Development of the class as a community is critical. In a community, trust and respect are shared by everyone. Traditionally, respect was reserved for the teacher: the teacher spoke, learners listened, and the teacher always had the last word. For a community to function well, all members must respect one another. Everyone's ideas deserve attention, and each person must be trusted to be responsible for the task at hand. Everyone must be trusted to be able to learn. In the beginning of the year, teachers need to work hard establishing routines and structures for math workshop. The learners in their charge must be led to trust that their ideas count, that their peers and the teacher really care about their thinking, that they will be given the time to explore different strategies and pursue their inquiries, that their questions and insights matter.

But community cannot be divorced from content. Mathematicians talk about mathematical ideas, not feelings or rules of behavior. They respect one another for the mathematical ideas they bring to the discussion. Learners, no matter how young, know when they are really being listened to. They know when they are learning and when they are not. They know when what they are doing is interesting, when it matters, and when it is simply about pleasing the teacher. When intriguing contexts are being explored and mathematical big ideas are being grappled with, engagement is high. Children can be mathematicians when teachers give them a chance to mathematize *their* reality and trust that they can.

3 | DEVELOPING MULTIPLICATION STRATEGIES AND BIG IDEAS

. . . what a wealth, what a grandeur of thought may spring from what slight beginnings.
—H. F. Baker, on the concept of grouping

Wherever groups disclosed themselves, or could be introduced, simplicity crystallized out of comparative chaos.
—Eric Temple Bell

Buying fresh fruits and vegetables in New York City is very convenient. All along the streets, vendors set up their wares, and passersby frequently stop to purchase whatever strikes their fancy. There are so many of these vendors in Chinatown that they encroach on one another and on the lanes of traffic. The hustle and bustle of crowds of tourists and shoppers, and the many exotic smells and colors of flowers, fruits, and vegetables, make a walk through this section of the city an exciting journey.

It's also a wonderful arena in which to work on multiplication. Because the vegetables and fruits are often displayed in crates and boxes that form arrays (an arrangement in rows and columns), and because the quantities are often too numerous to count by ones, the vendors on a Chinatown street are a wonderful context for math investigations. To introduce the topic of multiplication, we asked third graders to figure out how many plums, lemons, apples, tomatoes, and so on, a nearby grocer might have on display (Kerekes and Fosnot 1998). We showed the students pictures of different arrays of fruits in boxes and told them a story about the grocer. The plums in Figure 3.1 are one example. Except for two children who had already been taught the multiplication fact ($6 \times 9 = 54$) at home, all the children counted by ones. Even though the plums were arranged in an array of 6×9, no one added nine six times.

Why did they all need to count by ones? Wouldn't it be nice if children could solve this problem by doing 6×10 and then subtracting 6? Or by doubling 3×9? Or at least with repeated addition or skip counting? How do we help children develop strategies like these? And perhaps even more basic, what does it mean to multiply? What strategies and big ideas do children need to construct with regard to multiplication?

DESCRIBING THE LANDSCAPE

Strategies

When children are attempting to understand "how many" (how many plums there are in the grocer's box, for example), the initial strategy they use most often is counting. They tag and count each object once and only once. This strategy in and of itself is, of course, no mean feat—see the first book in this series (Fosnot and Dolk 2001) for a detailed discussion of the development of counting and early number sense.

But counting by ones is not multiplication. The progression of strategies, or "progressive schematization" as Treffers (1987) calls it, from counting by ones to using multiplication, goes through various stages of development. Let's look at a few examples of the development of children's multiplication and division strategies.

Elijah is asked how many cookies there are in total in three bags of cookies that hold six cookies each.

"Six in each bag, right?" Elijah clarifies.

"Yes," the interviewer responds.

Elijah carefully counts out six light-blue Unifix cubes: "One, two, three, four, five, six." Then he takes a second handful and lays out another six, again saying, "One, two, three, four, five, six." Repeating this action a third time, he makes a third group. Then he takes three dark-blue Unifix cubes and lays one at the top of each pile. "These cookies go in this bag," he explains, demonstrating with his finger that the differently colored cube is the bag. Last, he counts all the light-blue cubes, beginning at 1 and ending at 18.

Elijah first counts each group separately and then counts the whole over again. When he finishes, he has counted four times—each of the parts and

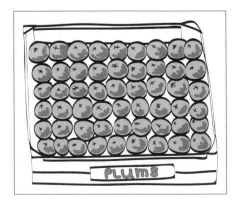

FIGURE 3.1
6 × 9 Array of Plums

the whole! Further, he needs to represent the bags with a different-colored cube. He appears unable to consider the six cookies as one bag. This understanding that six can simultaneously be one, one bag of six cookies—that what he has in front of him is three groups of six—is the big idea of unitizing. Piaget (1965), Steffe et al. (1983), and Kamii, Dominick, and DeClark (1997) all describe how number must be treated differently when it is unitized, a difficult idea for children. Prior to constructing this idea, number is used to represent single units—six represents six cookies. To understand that this group can be counted simultaneously as one requires a higher-order treatment of number in which groups are counted as well as the objects in the group:

> [Multiplication] requires the construction of new, higher-order numbers out of addition. In other words, the progress from repeated addition to multiplication requires the construction of new elements, through reflective abstraction, rather than the mere reorganization of elements that already exist. (Kamii, Dominick, and DeClark 1997, 10)

As children investigate multiplicative contexts, their initial strategy of counting by ones becomes inefficient (particularly when it requires counting four times, like Elijah does). Because this strategy is so tedious, children construct better ways to keep track.

Let's look at Richard's thinking when he is asked to figure out the same problem. He explains, "I went six, twelve, eighteen. I kept track by using my fingers."

Although Richard is keeping track of the groups with his fingers, he is still focused primarily on counting the objects. This strategy of *skip counting* is more advanced than Elijah's *counting-by-ones* strategy.

Contrast these strategies with Nellie's and Cleo's. Nellie is asked the same cookie problem: How many cookies are there in three bags that each hold six? She explains, "I added six plus six. That was twelve. Six more is eighteen." Nellie uses *repeated addition*. The same thinking is apparent in Cleo's strategy as she figures out how many cookies there are in four boxes each containing eight cookies. Cleo draws four slashes and says, "I'm putting four marks for the boxes. Eight plus eight is sixteen, and sixteen and sixteen is thirty-two." Cleo needs to mark both the boxes and the cookies, but rather than using repeated addition, she uses a *doubling* strategy. Hannah's thinking as she figures out how many toy turtles there are in five boxes containing seven turtles each, is remarkably different. She says: "I think about taking two from each box. Now I have five fives . . . five, ten, fifteen, twenty, twenty-five. Five times two equals ten. I add this to the twenty-five and that makes thirty-five."

Note Hannah's language. She says "five fives." She unitizes the units. She makes sets of fives and sets of twos and counts them. She has constructed the big idea of *unitizing*.

Hannah's strategy also makes use of the *distributive property*. Although she does not write it this way, she is doing $(5 \times 5) + (5 \times 2) = 5 \times 7$. This strategy will take her a long way as she attempts to make the multiplication facts something she automatically knows and when she attempts to multiply double-digit numbers.

Big Ideas

Underlying the developmental progression of these strategies is the construction of some major big ideas. We've already discussed *unitizing,* which requires that children use number to count not only objects but also groups. The whole is thus seen as a number of groups of a number of objects—for example, four groups of six, or 4×6. The parts together become the new whole, and the parts (the groups) and the whole can be considered simultaneously. The relationship of these parts to the whole explains the reciprocal relationship between division and multiplication. Because we know the parts (the number of objects in each group and the number of groups), we can figure out the whole. If we know the whole and one part (the number of groups, say), we can figure out the other part (the number of the objects in the group). Unitizing is also a central organizing idea in mathematics because it underlies the understanding of place value: ten objects are one ten. And it is at the heart of the idea of exponents.

Understanding the *distributive property* is another big idea. Realizing that 9×5 can be solved by adding 5×5 and $4 \times 5,$ or any combination of groups of five that add up to nine groups, involves understanding about the structure of the part/whole relationships involved (Piaget 1965). Here the nine groups are the whole, and the parts can be five groups and four groups, or six groups and three groups, or seven groups and two groups, and so on. Compensation is involved: as we gain one group, we lose another. The five becomes a six, but the four becomes a three ($5 + 4 = 9$, or $6 + 3 = 9$). Reversibility is also apparent: if $5 + 4 = 9$, then $9 - 5 = 4$. When using the distributive property, learners have to think about how to decompose the whole into groups: If one starts with five groups, how many more groups does one need to make nine groups? The distributive property is also a central organizing idea in mathematics; it is the basis for the multiplication algorithm with whole numbers—$12 \times 13 = (2 \times 3) + (2 \times 10) + (10 \times 3) + (10 \times 10)$—and in algebra—$(x + 2)(x + 3) = x^2 + 3x + 2x + 6$.

Understanding the *associative property*—$(2 \times 3) \times 5 = 2 \times (3 \times 5)$—and the *commutative property*—$5 \times 3 = 3 \times 5$—are also big ideas. Here's how one of Ginny Brown's third graders, Chris, explains the commutative idea to her classmates (Schifter and Fosnot 1993, 155): "We discovered that it really doesn't matter how you think about the problem because they're sort of the same thing." Chris lays out four rows, with thirty-one Unifix cubes in each. "See," she points to the length of the rectangle, "if you look at it this way, you see thirty-one groups of four; but if you look at it from the short side, you see four groups of thirty-one." Chris has constructed the idea that the array stays the same, even though one's perspective for looking at it may change. What was once a row is now a column!

These properties of multiplication can be seen and explored in a two-dimensional array drawn on graph paper (commutative property) or with three-dimensional boxes (associative property), but *understanding arrays* (and for that matter, volume) is a big idea in itself. Michael Battista and his colleagues (1998) describe the understanding of arrays as "spatial structuring." They interviewed several second graders and found that children go through a series of four stages as they develop the ability to coordinate rows and columns. Initially, students structure arrays as one-dimensional paths. Asked to figure out how many squares would fill a 3 × 7 array, one child filled the borders first, working along a unidirectional path. The second stage is characterized by structuring one of the dimensions (rows or columns), but not both. For example, children talk about the repeated addition in the rows but are unable to consider simultaneously how many rows there are. In the third stage, students become able to use the square units as indicators of how many rows and how many columns, but they still struggle to understand how one square can simultaneously represent a column and a row. Not until stage four are students able to consider one square as implicitly suggesting *both* a row and a column. The development of an understanding of arrays requires the construction of a big idea:

> Students' spatial structurings of arrays come as a result of their organizing actions (motor and perceptual) on the sets of squares. That is, students create spatial structures for sets of objects through the mental actions they perform on the objects. They do not "read off" these structures from objects, but instead, employ a process of "constructive structurization" that enriches objects with nonperceptual content. . . . This process actively establishes interrelationships between objects and is based on the gradual coordination of the individual's physical and attentional actions. (Battista et al. 1998, 530–31)

Just as students struggle to understand unitizing—how six objects can simultaneously be one group—they struggle to understand how one square can simultaneously be part of a row and a column. This idea is another central organizing principal in mathematics; it underlies the structure of the Cartesian coordinate system. Further, arrays are important models of multiplication. The relationship between area and perimeter—and between surface area and volume—relies on this model.

Big ideas involve structuring—understanding the structure and/or relationship between the parts and the whole. Because the construction of part/whole relationships requires a new perspective (e.g., groups can be counted as well as units), this development often is characterized by puzzlement (or *disequilibrium*, to use Piaget's term), exploration, collecting data, searching for patterns, and investigating why the patterns occur. The strategies that children (or for that matter all human beings) use are representative of the structures—the big ideas—they have constructed.

But there is also interplay between strategies and big ideas—or schemes and structures. Sometimes a new strategy is attempted without the learner's understanding why it works. Sometimes, when the strategy is explored to see whether it will always work, and when the learner comes to understand why it works, a big idea is constructed. Other times the idea comes first and the strategy follows. Learning, in general, is a case of refining schemes and grappling with big ideas. Both schemes and big ideas need to be constructed, and their effect on each other is reciprocal.

FACILITATING THE JOURNEY

Minilessons Using Pictures

The children we observed earlier in this chapter used several strategies: counting by ones (Elijah), skip counting (Richard), doubling (Nellie), and the distributive property (Cleo). As teachers, how can we facilitate the development of these strategies? Initially, children count by ones. How do we help children construct efficient multiplication strategies?

Compare the pictures of the apples, lemons, and tomatoes in Figure 3.2 with the picture of the plums in Figure 3.1. They are all arranged in arrays, but the apples, lemons, and tomatoes are smaller quantities. The array of apples has only three in each row and two in each column; the array of lemons, three and three. Quantities of five or less can usually be *subitized*— perceived as a whole without doing any mathematical thinking. Therefore, the pictures in Figure 3.2 subtly suggest skip counting. Of course, children who need to count by ones can. The pictures are open; there is no one right strategy. But because arrays are used, arranged with quantities that are likely to be subitized, there is an implicit psychological suggestion present that may facilitate the construction of a skip counting strategy. That is exactly what happened when we (Kerekes and Fosnot 1998) used these pictures with the same children who had counted the plums by ones. To calculate the number of apples, some children skip counted by twos six times; others skip counted by threes twice and then doubled it. Some combined the crates visually and saw two rows of six; some saw two crates of six.

For our math workshop minilessons we use a number of pictures like these. Most come from curriculum material in the Netherlands (van Galen et al. 1991). We have designed others ourselves or photographed arrays occurring in a city environment. Some have potentially realized suggestions built in. Others have actual constraints.

Look at the curtains and window shades shown in Figure 3.3. Two of the shades are not all the way down on purpose. You can only count by ones if you count the objects on the narrow shade four times or those on the wide star-patterned shade twice. One curtain is purposely pulled back. This series of pictures is designed to support the development of doubling. Of course if children count by ones, their strategy will be accepted and discussed. But the built-in constraint is likely to point up the inefficiency of this approach.

When a classroom of children was shown the picture of the curtained window, none counted by ones (although four responses were unclassifiable), five used skip counting (3, 6, 9, 12 . . . 24), two use repeated addition (they actually wrote $3 + 3 + 3 + 3 + 3 + 3 + 3 + 3 = 24$), and eleven doubled 4×3. In the ensuing discussion, children explained how the eight rows of three diamonds could be figured out by doing four rows and doubling the answer. To represent what these children were sharing and to introduce the notation, the teacher wrote the symbols to represent this idea: $8 \times 3 = 2 \times (4 \times 3) = (4 \times 3) + (4 \times 3) = 24$.

A series of patio drawings, most with furniture covering some of the tiles (see Figure 3.4), supports the development of the distributive property. Here it is even more difficult to count by ones. The series begins with a picture of a 5×5 patio. Will children use this to figure out the second patio, partially covered by the beach umbrella—$(5 \times 5) + (1 \times 5) = 6 \times 5$?

FIGURE 3.2
Apples, Lemons, and Tomatoes

FIGURE 3.3
Curtains and Shades

Will they use it to figure out the patio with the chaise lounge—(5 × 5) +
(4 × 5) = 9 × 5?

Also note the potentially realized suggestion built into Figure 3.5. How
many muffins does the baker have? How many did he have when all the
trays were filled? How many has he sold? The muffins in the second and
third trays are related to the amount in the first tray. Will children notice
this? Will they use a strategy based on the distributive property, seeing that
9 × 4 = (5 × 4) + (4 × 4)?

Jackie (see Figure 3.6) still counts by ones, not realizing or making use
of the suggestion. Edward (see Figure 3.7) also ignores the constraint, although he employs a slightly more efficient strategy than Jackie's. He figures
out the problem by skip counting by twos. Wendy (see Figure 3.8) begins
by using repeated addition. She solves the second and third trays by repeat-
edly adding fours, but when she gets to the first tray she shifts her strategy
to the distributive property. She describes the relationship between the trays
and adds the second and third together to get the first. She also notes the total number of muffins the trays can hold. Sam (see Figure 3.9) employs the
distributive property from the beginning. He writes, "[The middle one] have
16 because the right one have 20 if I take away 4 it will be 16" (4 × 4 = 5

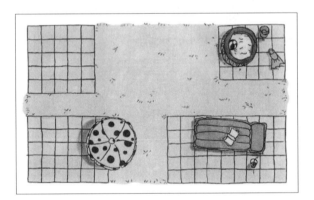

FIGURE 3.4
Patios

FIGURE 3.5
The Baker's Dilemma

× 4 − 4). And about the first tray he writes, "There are 36. The last one help me because I plus 20 more and I got 36."

Although the baker's problem is not designed to support doubling and halving, some children do use this strategy—see Amanda's work in Figure 3.10. She figures out that $4 \times 4 = 2 \times 8$ and that $5 \times 4 = 8 + 8 + 4$. She solves the first tray by turning 9×4 into $(4 \times 4) + (4 \times 4) + 4$.

Each picture gives children the chance to construct their own strategy. The important question for us as teachers relates to the role of context. Will children use their own initial, familiar constructions across contexts, or will they indeed change their strategy, constructing a new one in response to the potentially realized suggestions and/or constraints? If children do change their strategies, then using such pictures is a powerful pedagogical tool for us as we try to support and facilitate development.

By keeping problems open, we invite children to solve them at their own developmental level and we support their spontaneous, natural constructions. Suggestions and constraints within this open structure, however, may support the development of new strategies, because they make using initial strategies difficult, thereby facilitating disequilibrium. In this way they stretch and challenge strategies and enable progressive schematization.

FIGURE 3.6
Jackie's Strategy

FIGURE 3.7
Edward's Strategy

FIGURE 3.8
Wendy's Strategy

FIGURE 3.9
Sam's Strategy

FIGURE 3.10
Amanda's Strategy

Minilessons can also bring big ideas to the surface for further inquiry. For example, we might explore why the distributive property works by trying it out with larger numbers such as 16 × 16: What are all the different ways we could break this multiplication up? How are the parts connected to the whole? The students in Ann Denney's third grade have been working with several depictions of arrays and discussing how the numbers could be split. Now they are moving on to try it with larger numbers. Let's eavesdrop.

Josy decides to try to multiply 16 × 16. She splits each 16 into 10 and 6. Then she multiplies 10 × 10 and 6 × 6 and declares, "There. The answer is 136."

Cleopatra, who is working next to her, says, "That can't be right . . . ten times sixteen is 160—136 is too little."

Josy ponders this insight and agrees, although she is puzzled. "But what did I do wrong?" she asks. Neither girl can figure out the problem, so they bring their work to Ann. "Why didn't my way work?" Josy asks Ann, perplexed.

Ann calls the class together and asks Josy to share what she did. "Why didn't this work?" Ann asks. "She split the sixteens up correctly, didn't she? Ten plus six *is* sixteen. . . ."

"I tried sixteen times sixteen, too," Cleopatra offers. "Ten times sixteen is 160, and six times sixteen is 96. So we know the answer is probably 256." She shows the class how she added 16 + 16 + 16 + 16 + 16 + 16 by pairing sixteens and adding 32 + 32 + 32.

Josy agrees: "Yeah, we know 136 is too little, so we think you can't just split both numbers."

"Who wants to investigate this?" Ann asks the class. "Can you split both numbers when you multiply? And how do you know when you've done all the pieces?" Several children decide to join Josy and Cleopatra, and Ann suggests they use graph paper and make a picture of what they are doing. They set off with their materials.

Josy says, "Let's start with twelve times twelve first, 'cause we know that one." She outlines a twelve-by-twelve square on the graph paper. "I'll split twelve into ten and two. Here's the ten times ten." She outlines a ten-by-ten square inside the twelve-by-twelve (see Figure 3.11). "And here's two times ten."

"So what's left?" Ann asks.

"Two times twelve," Josy concludes, confidently finishing the array. "There, I did all the parts. It's 144. Now I'll try sixteen times sixteen again." She draws an outline of a sixteen-by-sixteen array and outlines the ten-by-ten within it (see Figure 3.12). "And here's a ten-by-six and a six-by-sixteen," she continues drawing in the parts.

"But you had a six times six before, didn't you?" Ann inquires. "Where is that?"

At first Josy looks perplexed, but then she sees it. "Oh, here it is!" she says and draws it in. "It's this little square! So I left out these other parts before!" she exclaims as she points to the two six-by-ten arrays.

"Is there a little piece like that in the twelve-by-twelve?" Ann asks. "You have four arrays here [*in the sixteen-by-sixteen*] and four numbers when you split each number, two tens and two sixes."

"Oh, yeah . . . a two-by-two!" Josy beams, proud of herself. "You *can* do it by splitting both numbers!"

Because Josy owned the question, she persisted. Because her dilemma was intriguing and meaningful to her classmates, they joined her. Often the best question comes from the child, and teachers just need to listen intently and trust. Josy is engaged in real mathematics. She has raised an important question: Can both numbers be split when multiplying? As she sets to work to prove it is not possible, she proves it is! Historically, some of the best mathematics has been invented this way.

FIGURE 3.11
Josy and Cleopatra's Array for 12 × 12

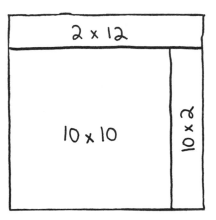

FIGURE 3.12
Josy and Cleopatra's Array for 16 × 16

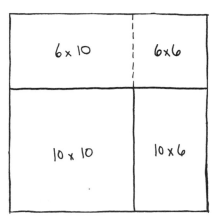

Investigating Boxes

Although minilessons sometimes spill over into inquiries like Josy's, most often they are short ten-minute starters at the beginning of math workshop. Minilessons can be designed to hone existing strategies or bring new strategies or big ideas to the surface for directed discussion and investigation. However, because it takes time to construct big ideas and new strategies, most of math workshop involves richer ongoing investigations.

Hollee Freeman had her third and fourth graders investigate how many different-sized boxes they could make that would hold thirty-six Christmas ornaments ($2 \times 6 \times 3$, or $4 \times 3 \times 3$, and so on) and how much cardboard would be needed for each one. As children began to build "boxes" with multilink cubes (which they used to represent the ornaments), they quickly discovered that although some boxes seemed different, it really depended on how you turned the box. For example a box with dimensions of four by three by three could hold three layers of twelve, but when turned on its side, it could also be a box that would hold four layers of nine—it just depended on which side you made the base. To develop an understanding of the associative and commutative properties, Hollee suggested that the children trace the base on graph paper to keep track of their work. Next to the outline of the base, she suggested they record the dimensions of the box, putting parentheses around the numbers that formed the base. Let's watch the children at work.

Natasha and Juanita have their thirty-six multilink cubes arranged into a box with dimensions of two by three by six. On the graph paper they have drawn an outline of the base as three by six. Next to the outline Juanita has written, "$(3 \times 6) \times 2$. The bottom has 3 rows of 6. It has 2 layers."

Natasha looks puzzled. She turns to Juanita. "I'm confused," she explains, "shouldn't it be six rows of three? That's what I see."

Now Juanita is puzzled, "Where?" she asks.

Natasha shows with her finger the rows of three, explaining, "See, three, six, nine, twelve, fifteen, eighteen."

"Oh, yeah . . . but look . . . see, six and six and six." Juanita turns the box, making the sixes into rows.

"Hey, we're both right! Let's write both!" Underneath where they have written $(3 \times 6) \times 2$, they write $(6 \times 3) \times 2$.

"How else can we turn it?" Juanita asks. "Oh, I know," she exclaims, answering her own question. "We could make this side be the bottom!" She turns the box so that the three-by-two side becomes the base. "Now we have one, two, three, four, five, six layers!"

"Yeah, and hey . . . we can write it two ways," Natasha proudly declares, writing $(2 \times 3) \times 6$ and then $(3 \times 2) \times 6$.

Although the girls employed the commutative property in this specific case as they investigated whether the base was 6×3 or 3×6, they do not realize that still more possibilities exist. Instead they pull apart the cubes and begin to build another box.

"Let's make two rows of six," Natasha suggests. "How many layers do we need?"

They struggle to build more layers and then to stick them onto the original layer of two by six. (One of the problems with multilink cubes is that they are often difficult to snap together.) Eventually the girls succeed in assembling a box that is $2 \times 6 \times 3$. They record $(2 \times 6) \times 3$ and then $(6 \times 2) \times 3$.

"Okay, now let's turn it to a different side," Juanita suggests, and she turns it over to make the bottom six by three.

Natasha records $(6 \times 3) \times 2$ but then realizes it is the same box they had built previously. "Oh, no," she exclaims, "we did that one already! How could that be? This is another box. We only made two rows of six!"

At first, they are both puzzled. But as they turn the box around, they see how the same box becomes a $(2 \times 6) \times 3$ or a $(3 \times 6) \times 2$ or a $(2 \times 3) \times 6$.

"Look!" Natasha resolves her original puzzlement. "It just depends on which side you make the bottom!"

Creating three-dimensional arrays has allowed the girls to investigate the associative property for multiplication in a context that makes sense to them. They can talk about layers of ornaments, rather than the abstractions of area and volume. They realize that stacked layers can be turned to become new bottoms, that rows can become columns. It all depends on the perspective, on the pieces you work with first—a powerfully big idea that can be written algebraically as $(ab)\, c = a\, (bc)$. But most important, they have constructed this idea themselves!

Investigating Multiplication by Tens, Hundreds, and Thousands

Tens, hundreds, and thousands are landmark numbers, and understanding what happens to a number when it is multiplied is an important big idea in mathematics. This idea also has a tremendous impact on children's strategies. Even when the distributive property has been constructed, children will still not break up the multiplier into tens and units unless they understand the power of multiplying by ten. For example, when multiplying 12×13, there is no reason to solve it as $10 \times 13 + 2 \times 13$ unless we know the important landmark and multiplication pattern, 10×13. Otherwise, we might just as well solve it as $8 \times 13 + 4 \times 13$ or $9 \times 13 + 3 \times 13$. How do we help children notice the pattern that occurs when multiplying by 10, 100, or 1,000 so that they will use it? More important, how do we help children understand *why* the "zero trick" (as they often call it) works?

Kim Outerbridge, a fifth-grade teacher in the area of New York City known as Spanish Harlem, decided to set her students off on a packing investigation. She told them a story about her friend Patrice, a graphic artist working for the shipping division of a company that sells and ships base ten materials to schools. Kim's students had had little experience with these materials in their prior schooling, so Kim collected a large quantity of them from other teachers and from the Mathematics in the City project and piled them at the front of the classroom. She developed a story about how Patrice has designed a long rectangular box that can hold ten large cubes, placed end to end. He wants to convince his company's management to use it for shipping large quantities of unit cubes, sticks (tens), flats (hundreds), and large cubes (thousands) to schools, but he needs to know how many of each type of block can fit in the box. He also wants to design even larger boxes. Kim's students immediately offer to make a chart for Patrice about how to fill his current box and to design several other boxes holding larger quantities. Let's observe the class at work.

Taniqua, Joaquim, and Juanita want to determine how many sticks will fit in Patrice's box. They have stacked ten large cubes, one on top of another. "The little sticks . . . there's ten in a flat," Taniqua begins, "and ten of the flats go in the cube, so a thousand of these [*she waves the stick*] in each cube," she concludes with a flourish.

Juanita, her brow furrowed, says, "That's a lot! Why don't we try it?" They stack up ten flats next to a large cube to demonstrate their equivalence.

Taniqua says, "Okay, there's ten sticks here [*she points to one flat*], so that's ten, twenty, thirty, forty, fifty, sixty, seventy, eighty, ninety, one hundred sticks in the whole cube."

"Not a thousand?" Joaquim asks.

"No, a hundred," Taniqua acknowledges, then quickly tries to cover up her earlier mistake, "but then that's a thousand in the whole box!" Although Taniqua's initial miscalculation was the result of haste, a thousand does not at first seem unreasonable to her. Only by actually counting and physically comparing the quantities is she able to see her error.

Often when children are dealing with large numbers, they have trouble imagining the large quantities. To develop an understanding of large amounts, they often need to build the amounts and compare them. They need contexts that engage them in manipulating, imagining, estimating, or calculating with large numbers. (Other contexts we have used in Mathematics in the City include: How many sheets of eight-and-a-half-by-eleven-inch paper would we need to cover all of Central Park? The Strand Book Store advertises eight miles of books. How many books do you think they have? Can all the people in the United States fit into the state of Rhode Island?)

Joaquim, Taniqua, and Juanita continue to build and then calculate the quantities by skip counting. They record their results on large chart paper, and Kim asks them to share first when she convenes a math congress.

Taniqua is their spokesperson. "We figured out that ten sticks fit in a flat, so we counted by tens. There's a hundred sticks in the big cube." Kim records Taniqua's thinking on the chalkboard, writing, "10 × 10 sticks = 100 sticks." Taniqua continues, "There's ten big cubes . . . so that is a thousand." Kim writes, "10 × (10 × 10) sticks = 1,000 sticks." Taniqua looks at what Kim has written, nods her agreement, and then continues. "And then we counted by thousands to figure the little cube. There's a thousand in each big cube, so we decided that ten thousand little cubes would fit in each box." Kim writes, "10 × 1,000 = 10,000."

"I'll accept that . . . it makes sense to me. What do the rest of you think?" Kim turns the question over to the class. Many nod in agreement, but Carlos raises his hand. "Carlos?"

"We got the same answer. I agree with Taniqua, but I think there's another way to do it," Carlos says with excitement. "I noticed a pattern, and I think you can just remove a zero." He pauses, then continues, "See it's ten thousand little cubes, one thousand sticks, one hundred flats, and ten big cubes."

Kim writes Carlos' conjecture on the board and asks the class to consider whether or not they each agree. "Will this always work?" Several classmates agree that it will, but there are also several students who say they are not sure.

Lucrece, who agrees with Carlos, tries to convince them. "He's got to be right because, look . . . there's a thousand little cubes in the big cube. So times ten, that's ten thousands. You put on a zero because now it's *ten* thousands, not *one* thousand." Several children acknowledge her reasoning, and she continues, "And a hundred sticks fit into the cube . . . so times ten, that's *ten* hundreds . . . ten zero zero."

Lucrece demonstrates a firm understanding of the place value at play here. Although Lucrece does not discuss it, because in the case of 10×10 it is obscured, the commutative property also underlies this idea. For example, to understand why 3 gets bumped to the tens place in 10×3 one must understand it is equal to 3×10.

Because this is such a big idea for children to grapple with, most likely some of Lucrece's classmates still need more experience before they can really understand her explanation. No matter how clearly one child explains to another, the ideas cannot be directly transmitted with language—the learner must construct them. Often when teachers stop lecturing and begin to facilitate more learner talk, they tend to believe that if a child just explains it well, others will understand. If this were true, the teacher might as well explain it herself! Mathematics cannot be learned through transmission—we each need to construct that understanding for ourselves, and that requires inferring and setting up relationships. On the other hand, "accountable talk" in the mathematics classroom goes a long way toward establishing norms of what it means to defend an idea (Cobb 1996) and brings ideas to the surface for reflection.

Because Kim understands that her students need more time to explore these ideas, she continues the investigation, asking the children to design larger boxes for Patrice and figure out what they will hold. The first box they design is in the shape of a large flat and holds ten of the original box, or a hundred large cubes. The next size up, which the children label a *crate,* holds ten large flat boxes, or a thousand large cubes. In the hall, Kim makes a huge display of the boxes, lining them up right to left: little cube, stick, flat, big cube, big stick (Patrice's original box), big flat (their first newly designed box), and large cube (crate). The children label what each box holds and how they know. They also label how many times they multiplied by ten when they were calculating how many little cubes would fit. Thus, the smallest flat is labeled "10×10, or $10^2 = 100$"; the big cube is labeled "$10 \times 10 \times 10$, or $10^3 = 1,000$," and so on. Labeling the boxes in this way allows the children to notice that the exponent tells how many zeroes there would be—10^6 is $1,000,000$ (six zeroes). This display prompts another wonderful insight from Pedro a few days later.

"Hey, the shapes of the boxes make a pattern," he declares as he stands in front of the display. "It goes cube, stick, flat, cube, stick, flat!"

Cathy is coteaching the class that day as part of Kim's participation in the Mathematics in the City inservice professional development project. Overhearing what Pedro has said, she comments, "That's why we put the commas there. Every time the pattern repeats you put a comma . . . after the one in a thousand and after the one and the first three zeroes in a million. That's neat that you noticed the pattern. That's what mathematicians do, too, you know . . . investigate patterns."

"Awesome!" Pedro is elated over his discovery and has been enjoying the investigations Kim has designed. Knowing that Cathy teaches mathematics at the university, he asks shyly, almost with disbelief, "Is this really what mathematicians do?"

"Absolutely!" Cathy declares. "We solve problems, get interested in patterns, and try to figure out why they are happening."

Pedro walks off with a smile. Shyly he turns, tossing his words back quietly so only Cathy can hear. "This is fun. I'm going to be a mathematician when I grow up."

SUMMING UP . . .

Large numbers can seem like huge amounts to young mathematicians. But as the mathematician Eric Temple Bell tells us, "Wherever groups disclosed themselves, or could be introduced, simplicity crystallized out of comparative chaos." Constructing the idea of groups is not an easy task, though. Children have just learned to count large numbers of objects. To count these same objects by groups requires that they treat number differently, that they unitize the objects into a group that itself can be counted as one. When children begin to form groups, they often use skip counting or repeated addition strategies to calculate the whole. But in the words of H. F. Baker, "what a wealth, what a grandeur of thought may spring from what slight beginnings!" Soon children are exploring the associative, distributive, and commutative properties and noticing the place value patterns that occur when one multiplies by the base. Their number sense expands to include multiplicative relations and operations. Sixty-four is no longer only understood as sixty-four units. It becomes eight eights, or four eights doubled. It can be a box $2 \times 4 \times 8$ or a perfect cube!

4 | CONNECTING DIVISION TO MULTIPLICATION

The mathematician is fascinated with the marvelous beauty of the forms he constructs, and in their beauty he finds everlasting truth.
—J. B. Shaw

Structures are the weapons of the mathematician.
—N. Bourbaki

Just as addition is easier than subtraction for children, multiplication is easier than division. And just as understanding the connection between addition and subtraction is necessary to understanding the part/whole relationships in the structure of number (Piaget 1970; Fosnot and Dolk 2001), understanding the connection between multiplication and division is critical to understanding the part/whole relationships in the multiplicative structure. Once children have constructed the important big ideas about multiplication described in Chapter 3, they begin to employ multiplication strategies in division contexts. Because they initially build up from groups to the whole using addition, once they have constructed unitizing it is usually not difficult for them to see how multiplication is connected to division. Even so, it is not automatic; they need to mathematize related multiplication and division situations.

Multiplicative situations can be solved with either division or multiplication. But until children construct the relationships for themselves, their beginning attempts at division are similar to their beginning attempts at multiplication. They count. Let's look at two children who are being asked to solve division problems.

Jacob is presented with a scenario about Rodney, who is putting twenty-eight doughnuts on platters for a party. Rodney is going to place seven doughnuts on each platter and wants to know how many platters he will have. Jacob takes Unifix cubes from a nearby bin, counting out seven. He lays them down as if they were the doughnuts on one platter. Next he counts out another seven cubes and places them in a separate pile. Repeating these actions, he makes a third pile. Now he goes back to the first pile and begins counting the whole from one until he gets to twenty-one. Then he takes another seven cubes out of the bin, counts these carefully to make a fourth group, and rather than counting on, counts the whole from one all over again! When he reaches twenty-eight, he looks at the arrangement in front of him, counts the groups, and proudly proclaims, "Four!"

Jacob is using a *counting strategy*. In fact, he counts several times: first each cube in the group, then the whole, then the groups. He represents the problem with the cubes concretely, using them as doughnuts and making piles as if they were on platters. He uses neither multiplication nor repeated addition or subtraction. He does build up from groups of seven, but he needs to count the cubes in each group and the whole several times until he reaches twenty-eight doughnuts. Only then is he able to count the groups, or platters.

Jane is asked to figure out how many beads can go on each braid if twenty-one beads are shared evenly among three braids. She counts out twenty-one cubes, one by one, as she takes them out of the box. When she has them all in front of her, she begins to make groups of four. After she makes two groups, she realizes that four will not work; she then tries groups of five. After making two groups of this size she looks puzzled and shakes her head—she realizes that five does not work either. From the eleven left she makes a third group of five. Only then does she begin to distribute the remaining six cubes evenly among the piles. Finally all twenty-one cubes are in three piles, and Jane smiles broadly as she announces her result: "Seven."

Jane's beginning strategy can be characterized as *trial and error*. She randomly chooses four as a starting point. When that doesn't work, she tries five. She isn't able to shift her strategy to even distribution until only six cubes remain.

Neither Jacob nor Jane is able to consider the whole and the group simultaneously. Each begins with the groups and builds up to the whole. Jacob does not even start with twenty-eight cubes; he starts with seven and builds up until he reaches twenty-eight. Jane does start by taking out twenty-one cubes, the whole. But she does not distribute them. She starts with a random number (four) in a group and attempts to build three equal groups.

These strategies are characteristic of children's beginning attempts at division. They are additive, building up from the group to the whole. And they involve counting several times or trial and error. How do children come to develop more efficient strategies? What big ideas must they first construct? How can we facilitate and ensure this development?

DEVELOPING BIG IDEAS

Dealing Fairly Produces Fair Groups

The problems given to Jacob and Jane involve division; one is twenty-eight divided by seven, the other is twenty-one divided by three. But the problem given to Jacob is *quotative*—or measurement division, as it is sometimes called. It requires seeing *how many groups* of seven fit into twenty-eight. The size of the group (seven) is specified in the problem; Jacob must determine the number of groups. Jane's problem is *partitive*—or distribution division. It involves figuring out *how many are in the group* when the number of groups (three) is known. Because children begin with a building-up strategy, focusing on the number in the group rather than on the group and the whole simultaneously, partitive problems are often more difficult for them. While counting can solve quotative problems, partitive problems are initially attempted by trial and error.

What makes partitive problems so difficult? To understand that distributing, or dealing out, to a given number of groups produces equal or fair sharing requires that children comprehend the one-to-one correspondence involved. Further, they must consider the number of groups, the number in the groups, and the whole—all simultaneously! The part/whole relationships involved make this a big idea. Children frequently see adults deal playing cards out one-to-one, but that does not mean they understand that this strategy results in an equal number of cards for each player. In fact, they often need to check by counting to see if the resulting number of cards in each group is the same. Only by exploring many partitive contexts and reflecting on their actions and the results, do children come to construct a "dealing out" strategy.

Constructing the Relationship Between Partitive and Quotative Division Contexts

American teachers often tell children that division is nothing more than repeated subtraction. This idea not only is insufficient but also hinders children's ability to construct an understanding of the part/whole relationships in multiplication and division.

Consider the following sock problems:

1. I have $12; if socks cost $3 a pair, how many pairs can I buy? (Quotative.)
2. Socks are on sale at 3 pairs for $12; how much is this per pair? (Partitive.)

Both problems require that twelve be divided by three, but where is the "repeated subtraction" in the partitive problem? In fact, the actions (or strategies) that children use to solve these two problems are quite different. For the first problem, children usually proceed like Jacob did with the doughnut problem. They lay out three cubes in a pile and then build additional piles until they have used twelve cubes. Then they count the piles. They don't subtract; they add. If they have constructed the relationship between addition and subtraction, they may be able to understand how this problem can be construed as repeated subtraction. But repeated subtraction does not describe the strategy they use, nor the way in which they think about the problem.

In the case of partitive division, the connection to repeated subtraction is even more obscured. There is no repeated subtraction in trial-and-error strategies. Even when children construct and use a dealing-out strategy, their actions are very different from their actions in quotative problems. How do they ever come to see the connection between these disparate actions and develop the understanding that both of these types of problems are division?

Ginny Brown, a third-grade teacher in Massachusetts, decided to have her children explore this big idea by giving them two related problems to work on (Schifter and Fosnot 1993). One problem (quotative) required the children to find out how many floors there were in a hotel that had 240 rooms, 24 to a floor. The other related problem (partitive) required the children to find out how many rooms were on each floor of a hotel with 240 rooms and 24 floors. Most of the children solved the first problem by adding groups of 24 until they reached 240. But they changed their strategy for the second problem. Here, they counted out 240 cubes and distributed them among 24 piles. Although their actions were different, they saw that the numbers in their answers and in the problems were the same.

In the subsequent math congress, after the children had shared their solutions, the discussion turned to the relationship between the problems and the commutative property of multiplication. Ginny built a 24 × 10 array with base ten blocks and asked the children to find their solution in the array. For the first problem children talked about rows of 24, and the fact that there were 10 of them (see Figure 4.1a). This matched the repeated addition they had done. For the second they shifted the array 90 degrees and saw 10 columns with 24 cubes in each (see Figure 4.1b). This matched the dealing out. One round of dealing resulted in 24 cubes being used, and when the

FIGURE 4.1a
10 × 24 Array

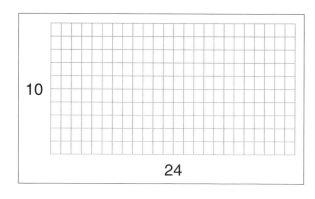

10

24

dealing was done there were ten cubes in each pile—now aligned with the columns. Understanding the part/whole relationships of this multiplicative structure allowed the children to generalize that either strategy could be used in both problems.

Jeanne Jahr designed a similar connected set of problems to generate discussion around this big idea as part of a pencil investigation. Jeanne had started the year with cans of pencils at each worktable, but they had been disappearing. Jeanne told the class that she was going to buy new pencils, since they were on sale at Ralph's Copies and Supplies, a nearby store. That night she bought 186 pencils. Before distributing them the next day, how-ever, she asked the children to determine how many each table (there were six in all) should receive. She also told them that the pencils had come pack-aged six to a box and asked them if they could figure out how many boxes she had bought.

Several students initially saw no relationship between the problems. They solved each one separately, often using different strategies for each. Leah, for example (see Figure 4.2), approaches the first problem with trial and error. She starts with 35, then 33, and writes, "to high of numbers [too high numbers]." She erases all her work and then tries repeated additions of 31. Finally, with much effort, she arrives at a total of 186. But to figure out the number of boxes, she uses multiplication. And quite elegantly! She em-ploys the distributive property.

Juxtaposing the problems did cause some children to think about the multiplicative structure, and the relationships involved, as they worked.

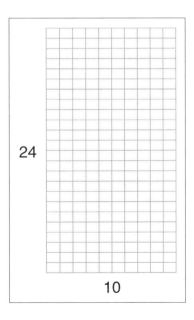

FIGURE 4.1b
24 × 10 Array

Isa and Connor immediately saw the relationship between the problems. Isa writes, "On paper I drew 6 tables. I dealed 30 pencils to each cuz 30 × 6 = 180. But to get to 186 each table gets 1 more. The boxes are 31 too. It's the same as before because the 30 at each table can be split into 6's.

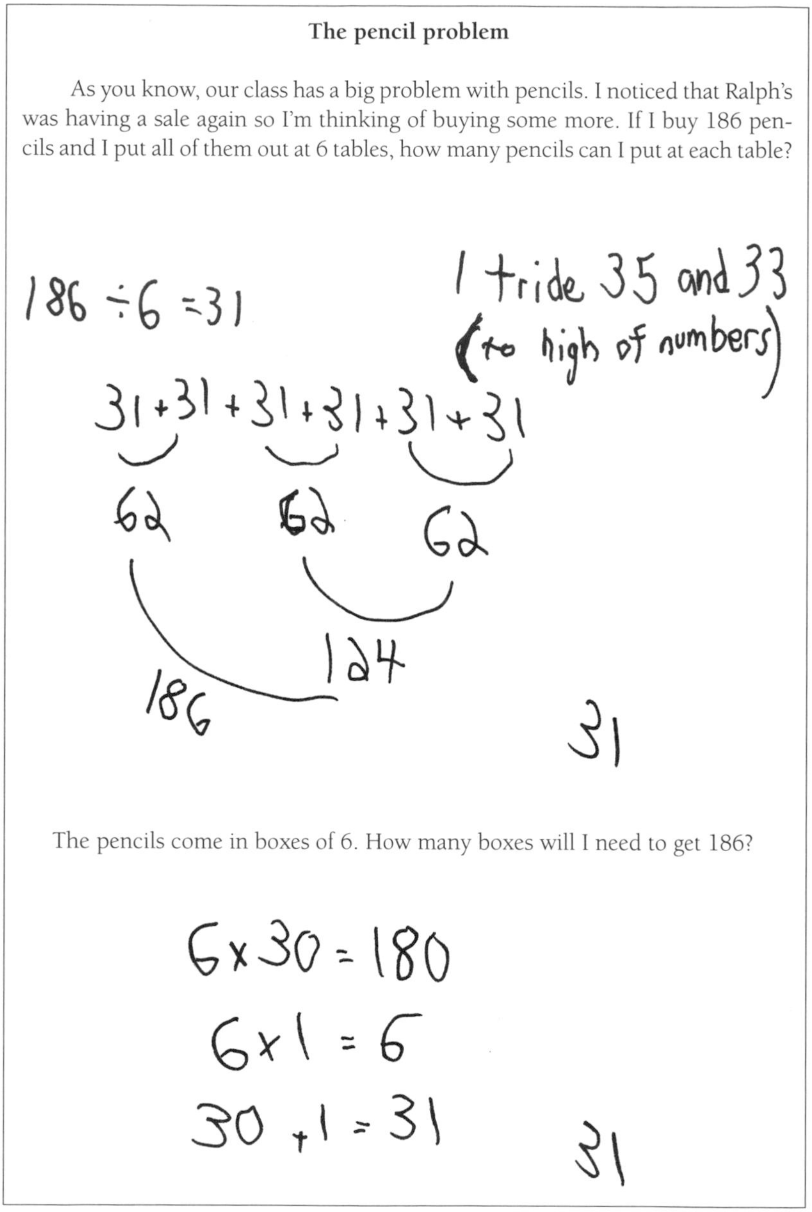

The pencil problem

As you know, our class has a big problem with pencils. I noticed that Ralph's was having a sale again so I'm thinking of buying some more. If I buy 186 pencils and I put all of them out at 6 tables, how many pencils can I put at each table?

$$186 \div 6 = 31$$

I tride 35 and 33 (to high of numbers)

$$31 + 31 + 31 + 31 + 31 + 31$$

62   62   62

186   124

31

The pencils come in boxes of 6. How many boxes will I need to get 186?

$$6 \times 30 = 180$$
$$6 \times 1 = 6$$
$$30 + 1 = 31$$

31

FIGURE 4.2   *Leah's Strategies*

You would get to 180, then split 1 box (1 pencil to each table) and you have the boxes equally split at tables." Connor solves the first problem by dealing out ten pencils, three times, to each table. He then completes the dealing with one more pencil each. He writes, "186/6 = ?" For the second problem he writes, "6 × ? = 186; 6 × 31 = 186 because 186/6 = 31 and 31 × 6 = 186."

Sam solves each of the problems differently, like Leah. But after solving both problems he writes, "They are exactly the same problems, but the first is division and the second is multiplication!" Because he has used multiplication to solve the box problem, he sees the problem as a multiplication one. Teachers are frequently tempted to tell children like Sam that both problems are division, but this is often confusing to children who have used a multiplication strategy. Isa, Sam, Connor, and their classmates are grappling with the important big ideas of part/whole relationships and the relationship between multiplication and division. When exploring part/whole relationships, asking children what they know and what they are trying to find out can be a powerful tool. Like Connor, they come to realize that in both cases they know the total number of pencils, but in one case they are trying to figure out how many in each group, while in the other they know how many in each group but are trying to figure out how many groups. Using multiplication and division interchangeably is powerful as long as children are clear what (the whole or which part) they are trying to determine.

DEVELOPING STRATEGIES

From Tallies and Pictures to Unitizing Groups

A second type of cognitive reorganization involves the refinement of a scheme or strategy. A search for efficiency is often the motivating factor behind this type of reorganization. As teachers, we can facilitate the development of more efficient strategies by building potential constraints into contexts and by discussing children's informal strategies with them. Let's step into a third-grade classroom in the Netherlands where Willem Uittenbogaard is the teacher. (These lessons were designed as part of an inservice research project at the Freudenthal Institute—see van Galen et al. 1991.)

Willem begins with a quotative situation that is meaningful to the children. The class is preparing for an open house at the school. The RSVP slips from the parents have been counted, and 81 people will be coming. Willem poses the question: "How many tables should we set up for the open house if 81 parents are coming and we use the big tables with six chairs around each?" As he presents the problem, he purposely draws a picture of one table showing each chair and then represents a second table with the numeral 6,

instead of drawing each chair (see Figure 4.3). By doing so, he suggests
some possible strategies, but he does not complete the picture and does not
try to lead the children toward the use of one image over the other. He
passes out drawing paper and markers, and comments, "You can draw, calculate, whatever you like." He then moves around the classroom, observing
and questioning, as the children work, draw, and talk out their solutions
with one another.

This is the first time these children have been introduced to division.
Prior to this lesson, there has been no explanation or direct teaching about
it. The topic is being introduced here by involving the children in a realistic
investigation. Will all the children be able to solve the problem? Only half
the class? What kinds of strategies will they use? How will they deal with the
remainder?

Nokolaus (see Figure 4.4) makes use of the implicit hint in Willem's
model. He draws a table with six chairs first, then proceeds to represent each
table symbolically as a rectangle with the numeral 6 as he progresses
through his solution. His work shows movement away from the need to
count each chair toward a strategy employing symbolization. Contrast his
solution with Ans' (see Figure 4.5). She also completes the problem successfully but she draws every chair and counts by ones.

Sabit (see Figure 4.6) solves the problem by counting on. He draws
each table and chair but marks the tables 6, 12, 18, and so on, which allows
him to keep track of the number of people seated as he works.

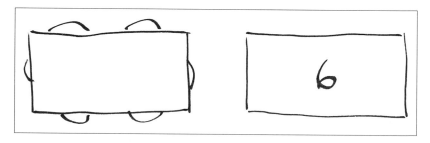

FIGURE 4.3   *The "Parents' Evening" Context*

FIGURE 4.4
*Nokolaus' Strategy
for the Parents'
Evening Problem*

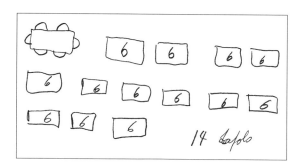

Norah's solution (see Figure 4.7) is very efficient. She uses the distributive property, grouping first 10 × 6 and then 4 × 6. Wesseline (see Figure 4.8) develops this strategy as she works through the problem. First, she starts with the repeated addition of sixes and then writes "24 + 6 = 30"; then she adds another 6 to get 36. Next, she apparently changes her mind

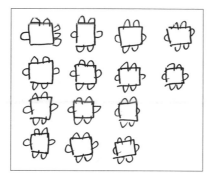

FIGURE 4.5
*Ans' Strategy for the
Parents' Evening Problem*

FIGURE 4.6
*Sabit's Strategy for the
Parents' Evening Problem*

$$10 \times 6 = 60$$
$$4 \times 6 = 24$$
14 tafels

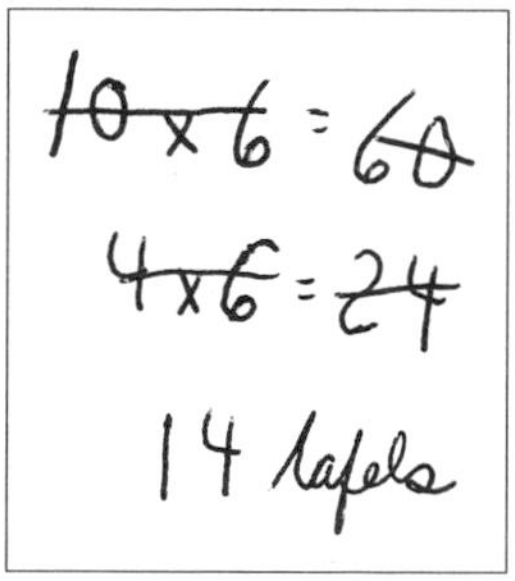

FIGURE 4.7
*Norah's Strategy for the
Parents' Evening Problem*

and writes ten sixes down; then she crosses these out and writes 60. She doesn't represent the grouping at the end, but instead writes all the sixes and a final three.

Every child in the class does solve the problem, with strategies ranging from those like Ans' (drawing every chair and counting), to those like Norah's (employing the distributive property of multiplication). Willem has successfully elicited his students' "conceptions at the start" (Duckworth 1987). Now he needs to begin the important work of stretching initial strategies like counting or repeated addition toward more formal, more efficient ones. Let's reenter Willem's class as he convenes a math congress, attempting to help his students become mathematicians in a mathematics community by exploring the connections among their solutions.

Willem begins by asking, "Nokolaus, what did you do? How did you solve the problem?" Nokolaus' strategy is close enough to a counting strategy, like Ans's, to enable all the children to understand what he did; thus, it will serve as a good entry point to the discussion. It is also a strategy that might stretch the "counters" toward the use of repeated addition.

"I drew each table and wrote six on it," Nokolaus explains.

"And you kept doing that, like so?" Willem adds more tables to his initial drawing on the board. "And then what did you do?"

"I added it all up."

Several children acknowledge that they did the problem the same way.

"How did you know when to stop drawing tables? How did you know when you had enough?" Willem probes.

Nokolaus shrugs and admits he had to count.

Willem wants to highlight the difficulty in Nokolaus' strategy. Repeated addition works, but how do you know when you have enough tables? He decides to ask Sabit to share next so that he can attempt to build a connection between Nokolaus' strategy and Sabit's.

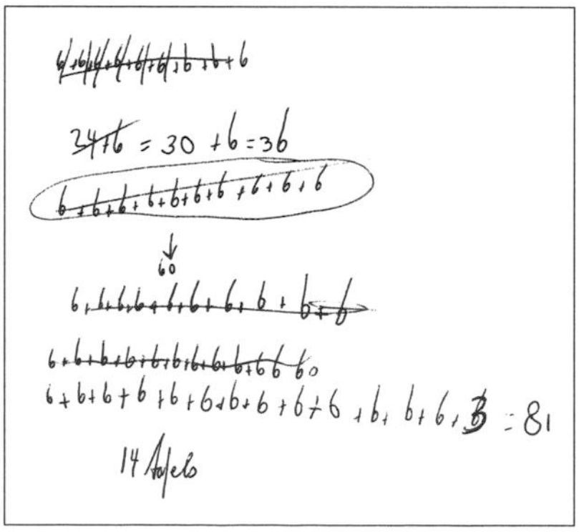

FIGURE 4.8
Wesseline's Strategy for the Parents' Evening Problem

Sabit explains that he "counted on" as a way to keep track as he went along. Although he has miscounted his strategy of "keeping track" (skip counting) provides a solution to Nokolaus' dilemma.

Now Willem looks for someone whose strategy might stretch the "skip counters." Both Wesseline and Norah have used the distributive property, but Wesseline's thinking needs some clarification, which Willem hopes will occur as she tries to explain her thinking to her classmates. "And, Wesseline, how about you? How did you solve it?"

"I did ten sixes all at once," Wesseline explains. "That was ten tables. I had twenty-one more people so that was four more tables . . . fourteen tables all together."

The children comment on Wesseline's shortcut, and Willem asks them to think about its efficiency. Then he suggests (only as a possibility) that they might want to try her shortcut strategy in similar problems.

The math congress has successfully brought to the fore new strategies for children to consider in future problems. Now he must design the next problem in a way that will promote the development he wants to take place. What problem might foster more efficient strategies?

Willem chooses a context that does not lend itself well to counting in the hopes of moving children like Ans, Nokolaus, and Sabit away from counting one at a time. Building a potential constraint into the subsequent problem, he asks the children to investigate how many pots of coffee need to be made for the parents if each person has one cup and each pot makes seven cups. As he presents the problem, he draws a coffeepot (see Figure 4.9). Coffeepots are not as easy for the children to draw as the tables were, nor is it easy to demarcate each cup. Willem hopes this will

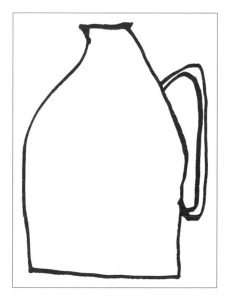

FIGURE 4.9
The Coffeepot Problem

encourage children to use symbolization and/or the distributive property of multiplication.

Valentia (see Figure 4.10) begins by drawing the pot, but she quickly gives up and uses numerals. With the earlier problem she had drawn every table. On the other hand, Sabit (see Figure 4.11) still draws all the cups. Some children just like to draw, and he may prefer this strategy for that reason, or he may just not be ready to give up his counting strategy. The context does not seem to affect his strategy, although the pot and cup handles do disappear and the picture becomes more symbolic as he goes along. Twice he even counts the coffeepot as a cup and only makes six other cups. He does not finish the problem, however, because the drawing takes too much time.

Ans (see Figure 4.12) really changes her strategy. She moves from drawing every table to an efficient grouping of 10 × 7. This is a big jump for her. Wesseline (see Figure 4.13) continues to group the sevens by ten, employing the distributive property, although she still represents each

FIGURE 4.10
Valentia's Strategy for Both Problems

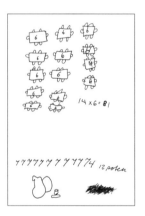

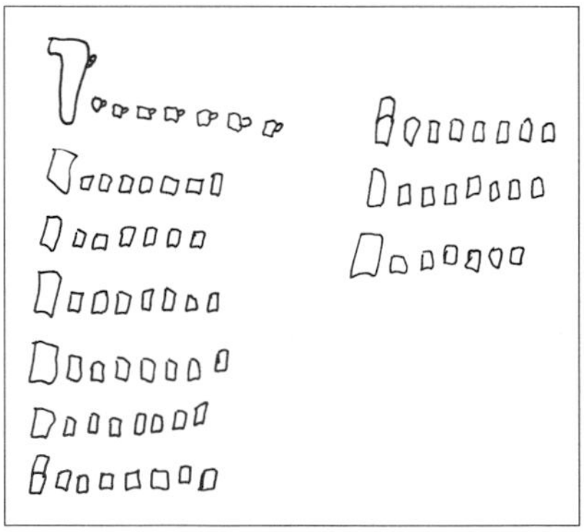

FIGURE 4.11
Sabit's Strategy for the Coffeepot Problem

seven. Norah refines her strategy so that it is nearly mental. She writes "11 × 7 = 77" followed by "1 more."

Although Willem's facilitation of the math congress and his choice of a context with built-in constraints does not cause every child to restructure his or her thinking, the children's work shows that a teacher can play an active role in facilitating cognitive reordering. Context design and the structuring of whole-group discussions are both critical in developing progressive schematizing.

Dealing with Remainders in Division Problems

Did you notice that no child had a problem with the remainder in either problem? Since they all stayed grounded in the context and dealt with the problems realistically, they treated the remainders sensibly fourteen tables need to be set up, even though one will not have six people; enough coffee is needed for eighty-one people, so we need to make twelve pots.

In real life, most division problems have remainders that need to be dealt with in context. Children need to encounter lots of problems in which the context affects the remainder differently. The Mathematics in the City program uses contexts like the following:

1. Everyone in our school—372 people, including teachers and students—is going on a field trip. Each bus holds 50 people. How many buses shall we order? (Remainders get rounded up.)
2. CDs are on sale for $12. I have $40 in my pocket. How many can I buy? (Remainders get rounded down.)
3. Our school ordered 300 pounds of clay, and the clay needs to be distributed equally among 18 classrooms. How many pounds of clay should each classroom get? (Remainders get divided evenly.)

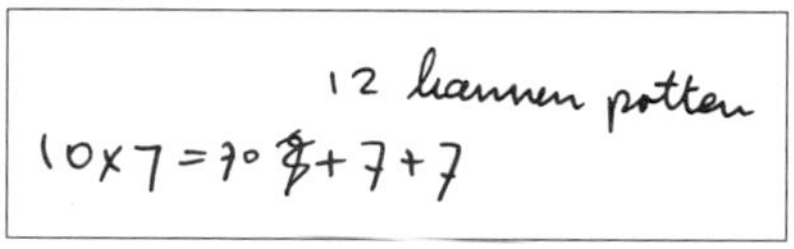

FIGURE 4.12
Ans' Strategy for the Coffeepot Problem

FIGURE 4.13   *Wesseline's Strategy for the Coffeepot Problem*

Children who are used to doing problems like these see mathematics as mathematizing. They find ways to think about their lives mathematically. They do not perform procedures that are nonsensical to them, and they treat remainders in relation to the context.

From Repeated Addition and Subtraction to Using Multiplication

Sometimes even the simplest of problems can be a surprisingly rich context for mathematizing. As a consultant to teachers in Columbia, Missouri, Cathy was meeting one morning with a fourth-grade teacher, Kristen Eagleburger, to discuss Kristen's plans and goals for math workshop that day. Kristen had been working on division with her children and had designed a quotative context about a friend who had recently made $328 selling SEGA games for $8 apiece at a tag sale. Kristen intended to ask her fourth graders to figure out how many games he had sold, then use the math congress to discuss the efficiency of their strategies. Cathy felt that while Kristen's content goals seemed clear and well founded, the context she had designed seemed more like a trivial "school type" word problem than a rich context that would be real and meaningful to the children—and one that might promote mathematizing. Kristen disagreed and wanted to try it anyway, and was Cathy ever wrong! Let's listen in.

"So let me tell you about my weekend," Kristen begins, the children grouped around her in the meeting area of the classroom. "My friend Sam is moving to Kansas City. . . ."

"Hey, I used to live there!" Heather interrupts.

Kristen smiles and continues, ". . . and so he was having a tag sale this weekend to sell things he didn't want to move, and to make some money to use for his new apartment."

"Hey, tag sales are fun," Nick interjects. "You can get great buys!"

Katie joins in. "We had a tag sale once, and we made so much money!"

Kristen is having a hard time getting out the details, but she enjoys her students' involvement and likes the way they are personalizing the story. "I know, tag sales are great, aren't they? Do you know how much he made just selling his old SEGA games? Three hundred and twenty-eight dollars!"

"Wow!" This time several children chorus their amazement. "SEGA games? What did he charge?"

"Eight dollars apiece."

"No!"

"Only eight dollars?! I wish I had been there!"

"How many did he sell? He must have had a lot!"

Kristen jumps in to raise the mathematical question she has in mind. "That's what I was wondering, too," she says, "and I thought maybe we could figure that out today during math workshop."

"Can we go work on it now?" Jamie speaks for the class. "I've got a way to start already."

These fourth graders believe the story. Although they have not experienced Sam's tag sale, they take it on as their own; in that sense, it is realistic. They begin to mathematize the situation. They set off to work in pairs. Several children use repeated addition, adding eights by doubling until they reach 328. A few children make tally marks on drawing paper, a very tedious strategy relying on counting these marks in groups of eights. Others use the distributive property of multiplication, making use of multiplication facts they know. Let's return to the classroom and listen in as Cathy directs the ensuing math congress.

"So, Carl, let's start with you," Cathy begins.

Carl comes to the front and posts his large chart on the board for everyone to see. "I made a chart," he says proudly. Carl has counted by ones but on his chart has written the multiples of eight (8, 16, 24, 36, and so on, to 328) as a way of keeping track as he goes along. "Then I counted all the numbers. He sold 41 SEGA games!" His classmates all agree with his answer.

"That's a great chart, Carl," Cathy says, acknowledging his hard work. "That must have taken you a long time. Your way, Noah, also took a long time didn't it? You were doing tallies, right?" Noah has drawn tallies on his paper and then circled them in groups of eights, and Cathy wants to build a connection between his strategy and Carl's. She also wants the boys to consider efficiency as the conversation continues, so she is subtly highlighting the tedium and difficulty in their counting strategies.

"Yeah, a long time," Noah admits. "I didn't even finish." Noah shows his work to his classmates. He has drawn and circled several groups, but drawing 328 tallies takes a long time, particularly when you have to count them several times to encircle eight each time. He had only completed 32 groups and thus did not yet have an answer.

"That's why I did it like this," Carl explains. "See when you get your first group, I put eight, then the second SEGA game is sixteen." Noah checks by counting his tallies and nods in agreement.

"Carl's chart is a little faster, isn't it?" Cathy points out. "Maybe as people share their strategies today we could look for ways that are really fast. It would be nice to make our work easier, wouldn't it?" Cathy laughs along with several of the students. "Keeping track seems to help. Jamie and Cindy, why don't you two share next? You had a way to keep track, too, didn't you?"

Jamie and Cindy (see Figure 4.14) have used a repeated subtraction strategy. Cathy asks them to share next because she wants to focus the discussion on the connection between repeated addition and repeated subtraction. As they explain how they subtracted from 328, Cathy finds these numbers on Carl's chart, moving her finger from 328 to 320 to 312, and so on.

"It's kind of like Carl's way, except we went backwards," Cindy declares.

"So we can keep track both ways," Cathy summarizes, "forward with addition, like Carl, and backward with subtraction, like Jamie and Cindy."

"But that's still a lot of work," Michael says. "Look how much paper you needed!"

Nina and Laurie agree. "Can we share next?" they ask. "We have a fast way." They bring up their chart (see Figure 4.15) and tack it up next to Jamie and Cindy's. Laurie begins. "We started to add up eights, but after we wrote down six of them, we realized that we knew six times eight. It's forty-eight. So we wrote that."

Nina continues, "Then two forty-eights. So that is . . . twelve eights . . . and we added forty-eight and forty-eight. That's ninety-six. Then we did another forty-eight, and another. We kept going like that until we got to 288."

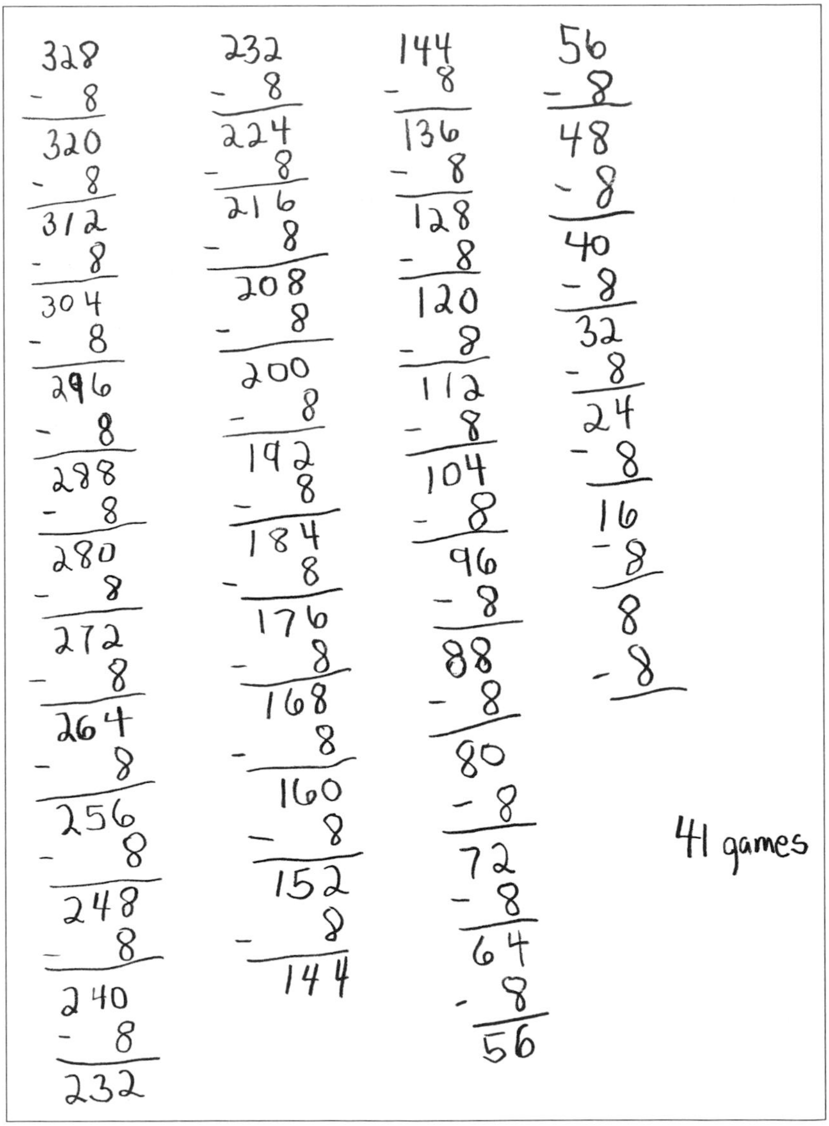

FIGURE 4.14   *Jamie and Cindy's Repeated Subtraction Strategy*

"Yeah, then we ran into a problem," Laurie interrupts. "We couldn't do another forty-eight, only forty."

"How did you know when to stop?" Cathy asks.

"Because we needed to get to 328," Laurie answers, surprised at Cathy's question.

It is often difficult for learners to understand the strategies that are most different from their own. Jamie and Cindy have subtracted. They knew to stop when they reached zero. But are they understanding Nina and Laurie's strategy? And what sense is Noah or Carl making of this strategy? "Noah, are you getting this?" Cathy asks. "Can you help me? Because this would be such

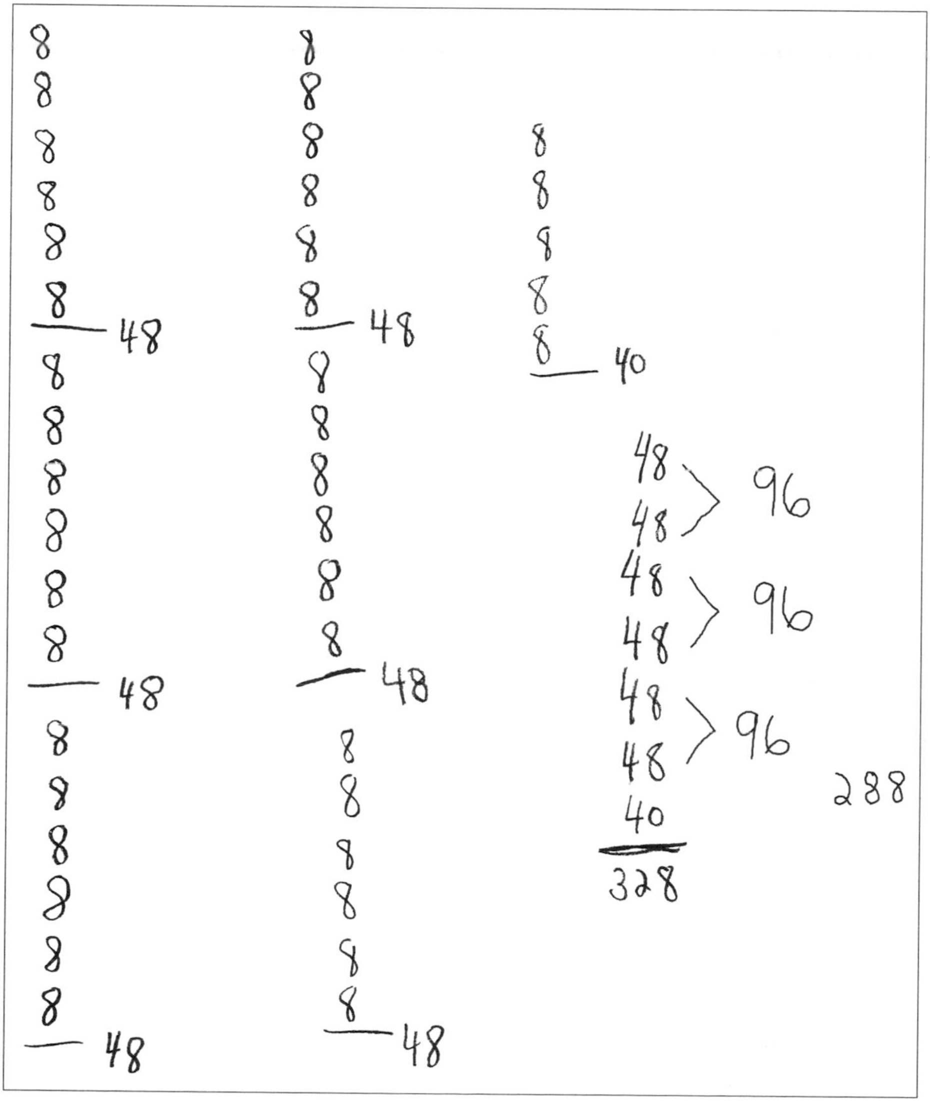

FIGURE 4.15   *Nina's and Laurie's Strategy Brings a Familiar Fact of 6 × 8*

a great shortcut, wouldn't it? It would save you from doing all those tallies, and it would save Carl from all the counting."

Noah shakes his head in bewilderment.

"Who thinks they understand?"

Jamie offers to try to explain. As she does, Cathy lays out six stacks of Unifix cubes, eight cubes to a stack, on the floor for Noah to see. As she builds the six eights and then the twelve eights she asks Carl to find the numbers on his chart. "So, Carl, when they got to forty-eight they said that was six SEGA games. How many is that on your chart?"

Carl counts the numbers to forty-eight and declares, "Six."

Cathy continues, "And what about the ninety-six . . . how many games is that?"

Carl returns to the numeral 8 on his chart and counts from there, finally announcing, "Twelve."

Interestingly, Carl cannot automatically see that if forty-eight is six games, then ninety-six is twelve. Nor does he count on from the forty-eight. He returns to eight, the beginning. It is so difficult for children to comprehend how number can be used to count elements in the group (the eight dollars) and the groups simultaneously. Carl is able to count each of the groups of eight as one. He demonstrates that well with his finger as he counts. His skip counting chart shows each leap of eight, and each leap represents to him a game. In this sense he is counting both groups and elements simultaneously. But Nina and Laurie are now treating forty-eight (6 × 8) as a unit. They are adding groups of forty-eights, and each of these represents six games! No wonder Noah and Carl are struggling to understand.

Cathy continues to try to bridge understanding. The numbers on Carl's chart are arranged across the paper in number-line fashion, and the Unifix cubes on the floor are arranged in rectangular arrays (6 × 8) of forty-eights.

"Is it all right if I write on your chart, Carl?" Cathy asks before she attempts to add marks to connect the strategies. Respecting children and their work is critical in a learning community. If we expect children to take pride in their work, we need to treat it with the same respect.

Carl nods yes, and Cathy draws a big leap from before the eight (implying zero) to forty-eight (see Figure 4.16). "So how many SEGA games is this, Carl?"

FIGURE 4.16
Cathy Draws on Carl's Skip Counting Chart

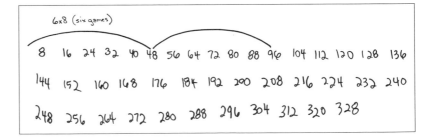

Carl responds, "Six." Cathy writes "6 × 8, six games" above the line.

"Noah, can you check him? Could you build it with the stacks of cubes?" Cathy asks. Since Noah had used tallies, the cubes are closer to his way of thinking. Each cube is like a tally, and the stack is like the group he circled. Cathy wants to ensure that Noah has the opportunity to arrange the six stacks into an array that can be connected to the leaps on Carl's chart. Cathy continues drawing each of the leaps that Nina and Laurie have made on Carl's chart, while Noah builds the arrays and checks the stacks.

When the representations are complete, Cathy returns to Nina and Laurie. "What do you think, girls? Does this represent your thinking?" The girls agree that it does, and Cathy asks whether anyone has a question for them.

"I do." Monica has been attentive but quiet during the discussion, and she looks puzzled. "Why did you do six times eight in the first place?" Several children indicate they have the same question.

Nina and Laurie just shrug their shoulders. "I don't know," Laurie tries to explain, "it just seemed easier. We knew six times eight."

"But adding forty-eights is hard." Monica doesn't let go. "Why didn't you pick an easier number?"

Monica's question is powerful. She herself has used 10 × 8—a much more efficient strategy, one that makes use of the place value in our number system. This is an important landmark for children to reach. But for children to see the friendliness of multiplying by ten, they must understand place value and the pattern that results. Otherwise, multiplying by ten is no friendlier than multiplying by six. Cathy wants to capitalize on this teaching moment. "Like what, Monica? How did you do it? Do you have a suggestion for Nina and Laurie?"

Monica brings her chart up. She has written "80 + 80 + 80 + 80." "I did eighties," she points to her chart as she explains. "So then I knew that it was forty-one games."

"I wonder where she got the eighties?" Cathy poses the question to the class.

Noah looks totally befuddled. "Maybe it was a good guess?" he asks.

"Was it a good guess, Monica?"

"No, because of ten it was easy. I just knew ten times eight was eighty. That's easy. So then I knew that it was ten games plus ten games plus ten games plus ten games. That was 320 dollars . . . and so . . . one more game. He sold forty-one games."

"That's sort of like my way," Michael pipes up. "But I did four times eight first. I knew that was thirty-two. And ten times that is 320."

Michael and Monica are using very efficient strategies. Michael's is the basis of the long division algorithm. Although it is tempting to encourage all students to use these efficient strategies, they need time to explore them and understand them for themselves. If learning is developmental, then it is an impossible goal to get all children to use the same strategy, attain the same understanding, at the same time. The learning horizon is efficient division strategies, but genuine learning takes many paths. Children need to build many big ideas and use many strategies on their way to this horizon (see Chapter 2). Cathy wants to continue this whole-group discussion at this moment, but the children have been sitting and discussing their strategies now for a long time. To continue would frustrate and bore many of the children who are not understanding what Michael and Monica did and who need more experience multiplying by ten and exploring the associative property of multiplication. The purpose of the congress is not to get all the children to the same point at the end but to explore connections among solutions—to challenge each child yet keep the community as a whole moving toward the horizon. Noah, Jamie, and Cindy may be challenged to use Carl's strategy; Carl may be challenged to use multiplication; Nina and Laurie may be challenged to use Monica's strategy; and Monica may be challenged to use Michael's. Other children may begin to think about using arrays and number lines to represent their work.

After the lesson, Cathy and Kristen planned together a context and several minilessons to move children closer to efficient division strategies. The context they developed for the next day was the following: At the store the SEGA games cost $22 apiece. If Sam goes to the store to buy new SEGA games, how many can he buy with the $328 he made by selling his old ones? This context may support more children as they begin to make groups of tens (see Figure 4.17).

To challenge a few of the other students, such as Monica and Michael, and to deepen their understanding, Cathy and Kristen planned a second situation: At the end of the day, the cash register at the SEGA stand contains $3,432. The shopkeeper wonders how many games have been sold that day.

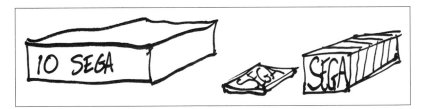

FIGURE 4.17
*SEGA Games Packed
Ten to a Box*

SUMMING UP . . .

Understanding multiplication and division requires understanding the relationship between them. Learners often mathematize division contexts by dealing out (partitioning) or by repeated subtraction or addition (in quotative situations). These actions are very different, and therefore it is difficult at first for learners to see how the problems are related. When learners build a multiplicative structure, they have a powerful form that allows them to mathematize situations with either multiplication or division strategies and to understand the part/whole relationships. A mathematician from the Nicolas Bourbaki group has written, "Structures are the weapons of the mathematician." These multiplicative structures provide young mathematicians with powerful new insights as they view their lived world through a mathematical lens. Even a young mathematician is "fascinated with the marvelous beauty of the forms he constructs, and in their beauty he finds everlasting truth."

5 | DEVELOPING MATHEMATICAL MODELS

The essential fact is that all the pictures that science now draws of nature, and which alone seem capable of according with observational facts, are mathematical pictures

—Sir James Jeans

The purpose of models is not to fit the data but to sharpen the questions.

—Samuel Karlin

WHAT ARE MATHEMATICAL MODELS?

When mathematics is understood to be mathematizing—the human activity of organizing and interpreting reality mathematically—rather than a closed system of content to be transmitted or even discovered, mathematical models become very important. It is impossible to discuss mathematizing without simultaneously discussing models.

Models are representations of relationships that mathematicians have constructed over time as they have reflected on how one thing can be changed into another and as they have generalized ideas, strategies, and representations across contexts. Although models are used as a lens when new mathematical questions are being explored, they are themselves constructed in the development of our mathematical awareness.

In a sense, models are mental maps mathematicians use as they organize their activity, solve problems, or explore relationships. For example, when mathematicians are thinking about number, they may have a number line in mind. They think about where numbers are in relation to one another on this line, and they imagine moving back and forth along it. A geometric model of number is another helpful mental map. For example, one might imagine 64 transformed into a square (8×8) and then into a cube ($4 \times 4 \times 4$), and 27 as a smaller cube ($3 \times 3 \times 3$), and then examine how these numbers are related to each other. Some models depict a network of number relationships based on benchmark numbers, their neighbors, and their use in operations. For example, a mathematician might see the number 64 and immediately think of 2 to the 6th power, or $70 - 6$, or 32 doubled, 8^2, or $128/2$, or $100 - 36 = 10^2 - 6^2$.

When a young child attempts to make lines on paper to indicate the tree on her street, she begins to model her world. The tree, as she has experienced it, is three-dimensional. She has walked around it, touched the bark, felt the shade from the leaves overhead. The lines she makes on paper are a *representation of* the tree on a two-dimensional plane to communicate to others what she knows a tree to be. The representation is not a copy of what she *sees*; it is a construction, within a medium, of what she *knows*. It is a creation.

Children's early models are usually representations of their interactions with the situation rather than of the situation itself. For example, when Jeanne Jahr asked her children how 186 pencils would be evenly distributed to each of six tables (see Chapter 4), Dean (see Figure 5.1), like many of his classmates, models the distribution process. He draws six tables and writes 10 on each to represent the first sixty pencils he distributed. Next he writes + 10 to represent the next round of sixty pencils. Realizing that he now has 66 left to distribute, he then writes + 11 on each table.

As Dean and his classmates participate in activities like these, as they are encouraged and supported in mathematizing situations, their models will go beyond representations of their actions and move toward more generalized models of strategies. They will move from models *of* thinking to models *for* thinking (Gravemeijer 1999, 2000). According to Gravemeijer (2000, 9), "The shift from *model of* to *model for* concurs with a shift in the students' thinking, from thinking about the modeled context situation, to a focus on mathematical relations." This is a major landmark in mathematical development.

FIGURE 5.1
Dean's Strategy for the Pencil Problem

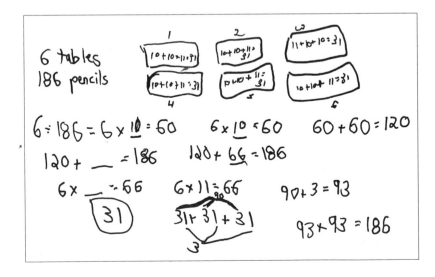

The Role of Context

In Chapter 4 we saw how teachers like Jeanne Jahr and Ginny Brown designed related problems in order to explore partitive and quotative division relationships. Juxtaposing related problems is a powerful tool for helping children explore and generalize models.

Susannah Blum, a Mathematics in the City participant teaching on a Fulbright fellowship in London's East End for a year, decided to use this strategy with her nine-year-olds (primarily of Bengali descent) to deepen their understanding of multiplication. Over several days, they investigated several different but related contexts.

The first one had to do with planning a Thanksgiving party for twelve other Americans teaching in London, to be held in Susannah's home. The invitations were to be sent out first class. First-class postage stamps in England cost twenty-seven pence apiece. The children helped Susannah calculate the cost of the postage. Almost all the children used some form of repeated addition. Shreena's (Figure 5.2) and Amsa's (Figure 5.3) strategies are representative of the majority of the class. Although some children (like Amsa) made minor calculation errors, all saw the problem as requiring repeated addition.

In the second context, a few days later, the children calculated the cost of the new pitch (blacktop) for a section of their playground that measured 27 meters by 12 meters if the company charged 10 pounds per square meter. The school's pool was also being repaired, at a cost of 3,500 pounds. Susannah and the children wondered which would cost more, the pool or the blacktop? Although the area of the playground blacktop, 27 × 12, can also be modeled with repeated addition, none of the children initially saw the connection to the stamp problem. Let's listen in.

"I'll make a picture," Saddik offers (see Figure 5.4). He begins by drawing a rectangle and placing twenty-seven lines across the top and bottom, and twelve on each side. Then he adds these quantities.

Ali, his working partner, comments, "But what about the inside?"

"Oh, yeah, I forgot," admits Saddik, and he continues to fill in his picture. His difficulty in drawing the area as an array of squares is evidence of how understanding arrays as related rows and columns is a big idea for children (Battista et al. 1998). At first Saddik works around the edges and down the middle. Next he attempts to fill in the right of the picture, but he does not make the rows equal—some have ten squares, some have twelve. And the ones along the edge are disregarded. Tired of drawing each square, he moves to the left of the picture and uses a ruler to make a grid. The grid, while an advance on his earlier thinking, is still not related to the marks along the side. Interestingly, although the boys are working on graph paper, they do not think to use the lines of the paper. And now they have so many squares, they have difficulty counting each one and keeping track.

"Wait, I'll make a new picture." Ali makes a new rectangle and draws twenty-seven short lines in each row (see Figure 5.5). "There's got to be twenty-seven squares in each row." Although he draws twenty-seven tallies for each row, his lines do not form columns. He understands the repeated addition, but he does not yet understand that the sixth square in any row must be in the sixth column. This relationship is the basis to understanding Cartesian coordinates. He does not yet understand how the rows

FIGURE 5.2
Shreena's Repeated Addition Strategy

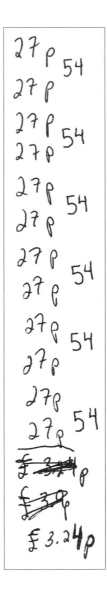

and columns are coordinated. Nevertheless, the boys have now modeled the problem with repeated addition, and they add on groups of twenty-seven, skip counting and recording as they move along, but making a calculation error as they work.

At a nearby table, Hakim makes a similar picture with twelve rows of twenty-seven tallies. But when he adds them up, he also adds in the two twelves. He writes:

> First I put down 27 and another 27 on the other big side. Second I put the 12 on one side and then put the other 12 on the other side. Then I noticed something. I had to do the middle. Then I done the 27 metres on the middle because it was 27 metres

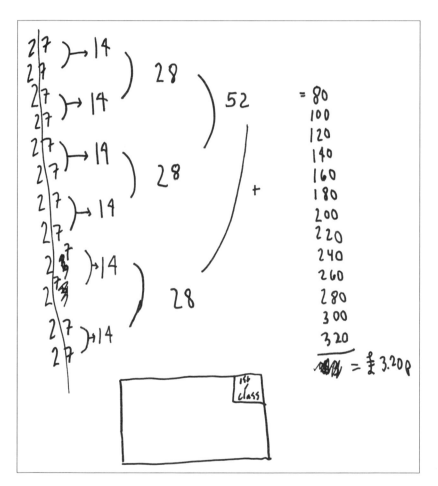

FIGURE 5.3 *Amsa's Strategy*

wide. Then when I finished I added them, including the 12s. Then I found the answer, it is 3,480 pounds.

Many children have made this same error. They have added the twenty-seven twelve times but they have also added the two twelves, not realizing that they have counted two columns twice. Arrays are difficult for children to understand. How can a square count *simultaneously* as a row and a column?

After the children have had sufficient time to complete their work, Susannah convenes a math congress. Having seen the difficulty children have had drawing and understanding the arrays, she decides to focus on repeated addition and also on how a square can be in a row and column simultaneously. "Ali and Saddik, why don't you start us off."

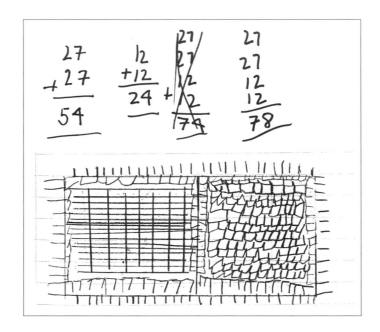

FIGURE 5.4
Saddik's Drawing for the Blacktop Problem

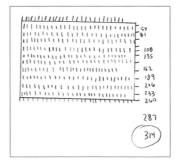

FIGURE 5.5
Ali's Rectangle

"First, I made a picture like this," Saddik begins, holding up his original drawing, "but then we realized that it was wrong. We needed twenty-seven squares in each row." He shows the second drawing and concludes with a flourish, "And then we added all the twenty-sevens up. So we know there's 314 square meters."

Several children look puzzled. Murmurs of disagreement are heard. "That's not the answer we got."

"You forgot to add the two twelves," Hakim says.

Now Ali and Saddik look puzzled. "Why would you add the twelves? The twelve is just how many rows there are. The twelves aren't squares."

"Moonifa and Scot, you disagree about this, too, don't you?" Susannah pulls more students into the conversation. Moonifa has added the twelves, but her **partner, Scot,** disagrees with her, although he is not sure. Rather than arguing about their computations, they each have made a detailed picture. Moonifa (see Figure 5.6) draws an array with coordinated rows and columns, but she draws twelve lines (rather than eleven) within the rectangle and thus she creates thirteen rows. On the bottom line she draws twenty-seven tallies, but three of them are not connected to column rules. Therefore she has only twenty-five columns. Scot (see Figure 5.7), because he is unsure, uses the graph paper so he can count. Susannah asks both children to post their drawings for the class to consider. Then she turns to the class and asks each child to turn and talk to the person he or she is sitting next to about whether they agree with the drawings and about whether or not they think the twelves should be counted.

Moonifa and Scot discuss their drawings with each other. Moonifa counts down her row of lines and then Scot's. Puzzled, she counts hers again. "What did I do wrong?" she asks Scot.

Scot counts her rows. "You've got thirteen rows," he explains.

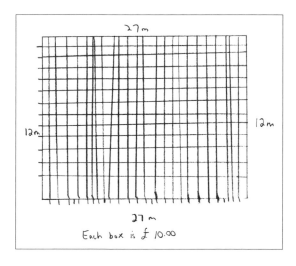

FIGURE 5.6
Moonifa's Drawing

"But I made twelve lines, see. . . ." Once again she counts her twelve lines.

"Yes, but you need to make squares, not lines. . . ." He draws a square in on his chart as he explains.

"Oh, right! The edges are like lines!" Moonifa smiles, recognizing her error.

Susannah now asks the other class members for their ideas.

Saddik raises his hand. "I like Scot's drawing, because with the graph paper I can see all the squares."

"Why don't we count each of Moonifa's squares and decide whether we need to add the twelves, and let's fix it to match Scot's drawing," Susannah suggests.

The children color in each square as they count it. Moonifa comments, "It's like each square is in a row, but the first square in the row also tells the number of rows."

"Right," Saddik adds, "it's twenty-seven squares across, but it's twelve down."

"Hey, I just realized," Moonifa exclaims with excitement, "it's just like the stamps! It's twelve twenty-sevens! So it is 324."

Generalizing the Models, Generalizing the Operations

Of course, models cannot be transmitted any more than strategies or big ideas can be; learners must construct them. Just because we plan a context with a certain model in mind does not mean that all learners will interpret, or assimilate, the context that way. But it is *likely* that a particular context will affect children's modeling and strategies in a particular way.

In a keynote address at the Exxon Educational Foundation Conference in 1999, Glenda Lappan told about an experience she had had as a teacher. After completing an achievement test, one of her students came up to her and said, "Did you see, the baseball problem was on the test?"

"Well," Glenda said, "I had seen the test, and there was no baseball problem on it. So I asked the girl what she meant. The answer was very in-

FIGURE 5.7
Scot's Drawing

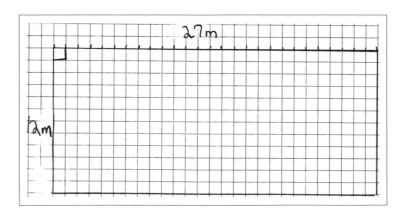

formative. This student had recognized that one of the problems could be solved the same way we had solved a problem in class earlier. The class problem had been about baseball. But the test item was not."

This generalizing across problems, across models, and across operations is at the heart of models that are tools for thinking. Models *for* thinking are based on the development of an understanding of part/whole relationships. This includes operations. To have a general model in mind when mathematizing, one has to understand the connection between the problems and the operations (e.g., multiplication and division) and one has to have a generalized notion of each that is not bound to the context.

Susannah's party-invitation and blacktop contexts have produced different models—repeated addition and arrays, respectively—and the children are beginning to construct the relationship between them. But multiplication is also the operation called for in combinations and permutations, and it can be helpful with ratios and proportions (for example, if a child who is three feet tall has a six-foot shadow, how long will the shadow of a nearby ten-foot post be?). Susannah wants to continue enabling these students to generalize multiplication, so she develops another context. Because the Pokemon game is currently a big hit with her students, she wonders how many days it would take for each of the twelve teachers in the school to play a game with each of the twenty-six children in the class if only one game is played each day. Would all the games be played before she had to return to New York City?

Shreena (see Figure 5.8), like many of her classmates, begins by drawing a connecting line from each teacher's name to a circle labeled "ME!" She realizes that this picture will be the same for each of the twenty-six children in the class: each child will have twelve games to play, one with each teacher. So she models the problem with repeated addition of twelves, twenty-six times. (Others add twenty-six twelve times because they see that each teacher will play twenty-six games, one with each child.)

Saddik asks Susannah for graph paper and draws a rectangle, labeling each column with the name of each teacher. Next he makes a column of twenty-six squares under each and labels each "26 children," forming an array in stark contrast to his earlier attempt in the blacktop context.

During the math congress, Susannah explores with her students how Saddik's array model can be used to show either 12×26 or 26×12 simply by rotating it 90 degrees. The children also discuss how the three problems (stamps, blacktop, and Pokeman) are related: how they can all be modeled with repeated addition and arrays and represented symbolically with multiplication.

With a group of third graders in New York City, Gary Shevell used the same didactic technique—juxtaposing contexts that are likely to be modeled differently but that will result in the same answer. He asked them to consider three situations: 4 boxes of crayons, seven to a box; the square foot of carpet needed for a closet, 7 ft. by 4 ft.; and the different outfits possible with four pants and seven shirts.

Almost all the children modeled the crayon situation with repeated addition and solved it by adding or skip counting. For the carpet situation, children drew arrays and then counted the squares. To make the outfits, children used a branching model, drawing lines from each pair of pants to each shirt. Some systematically produced all the possibilities; others approached it more randomly. Each problem was modeled by the children differently, and each was tightly connected to the context. Ana, for example (see Figure 5.9), drew each box of crayons and skip counted by sevens. She drew the closet floor with 28 squares in an array, but struggled to produce related rows and columns. Instead she laboriously drew each square, one at a time. To produce all the outfits, she uses connecting lines. When she had completed all the problems, she wrote, "7 × 4 = 28 because all the problems have that answer."

Noticing that all the problems have the same answer and understanding why and how they are related are two different things, however. It is easy

FIGURE 5.8 *Shreena's Strategy for Pokemon*

for children to notice that each answer is the same. What is important is that they grapple with the relationships—where the repeated addition is in each situation. An important landmark on the horizon is for children to understand multiplication deeply enough that each situation, regardless of the context, can be mathematized with multiplication—that each can be modeled with repeated addition, an array, and with branching. Isabelle illustrates the passing of this landmark when she explains in the math congress, "They are all the same. They are all 7, four times. Each pants can be worn seven times . . . so you do seven, plus seven, plus seven, plus seven. It's all multiplication!"

It is also important to develop a generalized model for division. As described in Chapter 4, some division situations are partitive, while others are

FIGURE 5.9 *Ana's Strategies for the Three Problems*

quotative. Developing an understanding of the relationship between the situations is important. (Seeing one round of dealing as a group being removed is a big idea.) On the horizon is also the ability to mathematize either a quotative or partitive situation with division, and to understand how both can be modeled with a number line, or with an array.

To support children in the journey toward this horizon, Susannah Blum presents two more related contexts, this time involving division. She wonders with her children how many loaves of bread the cafeteria must have on hand each day so that the approximately 300 children who take hot lunch can each get a slice. The loaves have twelve slices each. Because this context involves seeing how many twelves fit into 300, it is quotative. Her second problem is partitive and involves dealing, or distributing. The director of the school has bought 300 new red pens and wants the twelve classes to share them equally. How many should each class get?

Susannah chose the numbers in these problems purposely. She anticipated that most children would not immediately see the connection between the prior multiplicative situations and would probably struggle to do so even after solving both problems. After all, to understand the connection between the problems, they have to understand the connection between repeated addition, arrays, and combinations, and the relationship between multiplication and division. They have to understand the relationship between the groups, the objects in the groups, and the whole.

Devising rich contexts and playing with the numbers in the problems will not by themselves cause children to generalize. Some children in Susannah's class do not construct relationships between the problems, even though she has juxtaposed the contexts and numbers, and even though she has a math congress on these ideas. As adults having better mathematical understanding, we immediately see the models in the problems and we expect that the children should. But the models are not in the problems until we mathematize them as such. Children who have not constructed the relationships will mathematize the situations in relation to *their* insights, *their* strategies, *their* ideas. Nevertheless, juxtaposing contexts and playing with the numbers in them may invite some children to reflect on the relationships. At a minimum, Susannah is likely to be able to generate a "juicy" conversation on these relationships during her congress.

Using Arrays for Automatizing the Facts

Once children have developed an understanding of the operation of multiplication, emphasis is traditionally placed on memorizing the basic facts through repetitive drill and practice, using worksheets and flash cards. Is it necessary to memorize facts?

Certainly, in order to multiply numbers with double or triple digits quickly, we need to know the basic facts. But the debate in our schools often centers on understanding versus memorization, as if the approaches are dichotomies: children either count on their fingers or memorize isolated facts. Children need to understand what it means to multiply and divide before facts can become automatic, but understanding does not necessarily lead to this automaticity. In other words, understanding is necessary but not sufficient. Children often develop a good understanding of what it means to multiply two numbers, and they demonstrate this understanding by using their fingers, cubes, or drawings to depict repeated addition. Even with this understanding, however, they count several times—first each group, then the total. For example, to figure out 3×6, Elijah (see Chapter 3) initially counts from one to six three times and then combines the sets and starts over from one again to count the whole to eighteen. Even when children construct more efficient strategies like skip counting or doubling, they may still rely on counting with their fingers to keep track of the groups.

While these strategies are wonderful beginnings, children cannot be left with only these ways to solve multiplication and division problems. But is the answer to memorize isolated facts? How many facts are there? And how do we help children understand the relationships between facts, like $9 \times 7 = (10 \times 7) - 7$?

Common Multiplication Strategies

Children who struggle to commit basic facts to memory often believe that there are "hundreds" to be memorized because they have little or no understanding of the relationships among them. Children who commit the facts to memory easily are able to do so because they have constructed relationships among them and use these relationships as shortcuts. The most important strategies are:

1. Doubling: $2 \times 3 \times 6 = 6 \times 6$.
2. Halving and doubling: $4 \times 3 = 2 \times 6$.
3. Using the distributive property: $7 \times 8 = (5 \times 8) + (2 \times 8)$, or $7 \times 8 = (8 \times 8) - 8$.
4. Using the distributive property with tens: $9 \times 8 = (10 \times 8) - 8$.
5. Using the commutative property: $5 \times 8 = 8 \times 5$.

Memorizing facts with flash cards or through drill and practice on worksheets will not develop these relationships. When these strategies are understood and used, there are fewer facts to memorize. Using the commutative property, almost half of the facts are repeats. One times a number is of course the number, so these do not have to be memorized. Square numbers are easy for children to remember.

Memorization or Automaticity?

Memorization of basic facts usually refers to committing the results of operations to memory so that thinking is unnecessary. Isolated multiplications and divisions are practiced one after another; the emphasis is on recalling the answers. Teaching facts for automaticity, in contrast, relies on thinking. Answers to facts must be automatic, produced in only a few seconds; counting is not sufficient. But thinking about the relationships among the facts is critical. A child who thinks of 9×6 as $(10 \times 6) - 6$ produces the answer of 54 quickly, but thinking, not memorization, is at the core (although over time these facts are remembered). The issue here is not whether facts should eventually be memorized, but how this memorization is achieved: by rote drill and practice, or by focusing on relationships?

Children can make arrays on graph paper and, by overlaying these arrays one on top of another, explore relationships and write clues for themselves for the facts that are difficult to remember. Teachers can use pictures with constraints and mental math strings (see Chapters 3 and 7) to develop these relationships and strategies. In this way, the facts become automatic but the relationships—the heart of mathematics—are not sacrificed.

From Models of Thinking to Models for Thinking

An *open* array can be used in connection with multiplication and division computation, and while it initially is used as a model of children's strategies, it eventually becomes a powerful tool to think with. This is equivalent to our use of the open number line with addition and subtraction. Open in the sense that it has no numbers; the numbers in the children's work can thus be placed on it to represent their strategies—see Fosnot and Dolk (2001).

Let's enter Miki Jensen's fourth grade in New York City as she presents a minilesson on multiplication computation strategies using an open array model.

Miki begins by writing $2 \times 3 = ?$ on the chalkboard as the children cluster around her on the meeting-area rug. "An easy one," she smiles, seeing all the raised hands. "Lara?"

"Six," Lara responds, and Miki, using a small magnet, posts a cutout 2×3 array made from one-inch graph paper next to the problem. Next Miki writes $2 \times 30 = ?$; again, her students all raise their hand. Before she calls on anyone she continues, "Think about what the array will look like. Gabriella?"

"Sixty."

"What will the array look like?" Miki probes.

"Long and short," Gabriella responds. "It's thirty plus thirty." Miki affixes a 2×30 array to the chalkboard next to the problem. Gabriella continues, "You could do it another way, too. It's two times three. Then add a zero."

Miki smiles. "But usually when I add a zero to an amount I get that amount. Are we really adding a zero? Everybody . . . talk with your neighbor about this. What is happening here?"

Miki gives them a few minutes and then asks Charlie to start the whole-class conversation. "Charlie, I listened in on your conversation with Thomas and Taqee. Why don't you start us off?"

"We think there are really ten two-by-three arrays, but we're not sure." Thomas and Taqee nod their heads in agreement. Other children seem to concur.

"Well, let's check it out." Miki uses the arrays as a model to represent their thinking, placing the 2×3 paper array over the 2×30 array and marking a line at the end of each iteration (see Figure 5.10). By doing so, Miki begins the work of helping the children move from arrays where every square is drawn. Once the children agree that ten 2 × 3 arrays fit, she continues with her string of problems, writing 4 × 4, then 4 × 40. "Molly?"

"One hundred and sixty."

"I didn't draw a four-by-ten array on graph paper," Miki says, "so I'm just going to draw an open array—a rectangle without each square drawn. What will it look like? Will it be bigger than this other one?"

"It's four rows of forty, or ten four-by-fours," Molly responds. Miki draws a large empty rectangle proportional to the 2 × 30 (see Figure 5.11a). Next she writes 4 × 39 = ? and admits, "Yuk! This one's not so friendly!"

Olana offers a solution. "I did four times thirty first. That's a hundred and twenty. Then I did four times nine. Together they make a hundred and fifty-six," she explains.

Miki draws an open array of Olana's thinking (see Figure 5.11b). "So here is Olana's way. Comments? Is there another way? CJ?"

"I did four times forty first. . . ."

"You started with this one?" Miki interrupts, pointing to the 4 × 40 open array on the board.

"Yes. And every time I doubled the number, I took away one . . . well, not really doubling. I added it four times."

"You added the forty four times?" Miki clarifies.

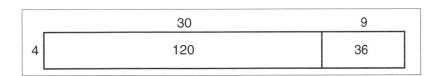

FIGURE 5.10   *Marking Ten 2 × 3 Arrays on a 2 × 30 Array*

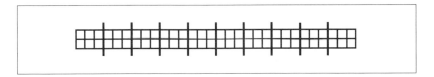

FIGURE 5.11a

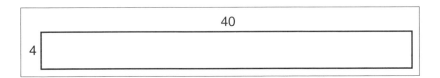

FIGURE 5.11b

"Yes. And every time I did, I had to take one away, so one hundred and sixty minus four equals one hundred and fifty-six."

"That's very different from Olana's way, isn't it?" Miki checks to see whether everyone understands. "Let me draw an array to represent CJ's thinking." She draws the array shown in Figure 5.11c.

Gabby now offers yet a third strategy. "My way is almost the same as CJ's. I used the four-times-forty array too. But I didn't think about four thirty-nines, I just took four away all at once."

Miki erases the lines in the array representing CJ's thinking, leaving the array shown in Figure 5.11d. "You just envisioned this? Pretty cool."

Each day at the start of math workshop, Miki continues her minilessons using open arrays and working on computation. She also launches more in-depth investigations, extending the array model to volume and surface-area contexts. For example, one week the children conduct an investigation over several days to find out how many different boxes can be made to hold thirty-six chocolates. The array model is extended into three dimensions, and area gets extended into volume. And the faces of the boxes become surface area, as the children explore how much cardboard is needed for each box.

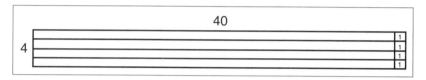

FIGURE 5.11c

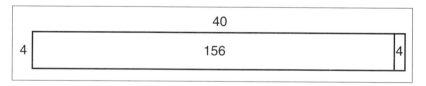

FIGURE 5.11d

SUMMING UP . . .

It is impossible to talk about mathematizing without talking about modeling. Mathematical models are mental maps of relations that can be used as tools when solving problems. These pictures, or mental maps, are powerful. The well-known scientist and mathematician Sir James Jeans once wrote, "The essential fact is that all the pictures which science now draws of nature, and which alone seem capable of according with observational facts, are mathematical pictures." These mental maps depict relations, and help us understand and represent our world.

Models themselves are constructed. They emerge from representations of the *action* in the situation. For example, children don't represent a tree as an object; they represent their actions in relation to the tree. Later these representations of action develop into *representations of the situation* using cubes or drawings. Eventually, modeling develops into a symbolic *representation of the mathematizing*, itself. Children represent the *strategies* they used to solve the problem rather than the situation itself. For example, they may use open arrays to represent their computation strategies, or they may combine arrays to help them remember and automatize the multiplication facts. As teachers work with children with models such as the open array, these representations of their strategies develop into mathematical models of number relations; they become *mathematical tools*.

The developmental process is characterized by generalization. The importance of generalization in learning cannot be overstated. Piaget (1977) called it "reflective abstraction" and argued that it was the driving force in learning. The mathematician Carl Jacobi, describing his own mathematical thinking process, said, "One should always generalize" (Davis and Hersh 1981). Each developmental shift produces a different way of symbolizing. The model eventually must be able to signify the relationships between numbers and between operations.

At the heart of modeling is number sense—the representation of number relations. As children construct mental maps of these relations, they are building powerful pictures of their world. As they construct mental maps they are developing tools to continue the journey of mathematizing their own lived worlds. And as Samuel Karlin stated so well, "The purpose of models is not to fit the data, but to sharpen the questions."

Arismetica

·OCVLI·

Monstrat ars numerū que virtus possit habere
Explico permumerū que sit proportio rerum

6 | ALGORITHMS VERSUS NUMBER SENSE

*We are usually convinced more easily by reasons
we have found ourselves than by those which have
occurred to others.*

—Blaise Pascal

*There still remain three studies suitable for free men.
Arithmetic is one of them.*

—Plato

Try an experiment. Calculate 76 × 89. Don't read on until you have an answer.

If you are like most people who are a product of the American school system, you probably got a pencil and paper, wrote the numbers down in columns, multiplied 6 × 89 (starting with 6 × 9, carrying the 5 and adding it to 6 × 8, for a partial product of 534), then multiplied by the 7 (starting with 7 × 9, carrying the 6, adding it to 7 × 8, then adding a zero to reflect place value, for a partial product of 6,230), and finally added the partial products (starting with the units), for a total of 6,764. To check yourself, you probably went back and repeated the same actions and calculations; if you got the same answer twice, you assumed your calculations were correct.

Now take out a piece of graph paper and draw a rectangle that is 76 × 89. See if you can find the smaller rectangular arrays inside this big one that represent the problems you did as you calculated. If this is difficult for you, the way the algorithm was taught to you has worked against your own conceptual understanding of multiplication.

Children make any number of place value errors in calculating each of these many separate problems, either in carrying the tens or in lining up the numbers. Why? Well, just think how nonsensical these steps must seem. Children of this age are struggling to understand that 76 × 89 actually means 76 rows of units (square tiles, say) with 89 units (tiles) in each row—in other words, the repeated addition of eighty-nine seventy-six times. As they treat the numbers in each problem as digits, they lose sight of the quantities they are actually multiplying.

Liping Ma (1999) compared the way Chinese and American teachers think about and teach the multiplication algorithm and how they work with children who make place value mistakes. Most Chinese teachers approach the teaching of the multiplication algorithm conceptually. They explain the distributive property and break the problem up into the component problems: $76 \times 89 = (70 + 6) \times (80 + 9) = (6 \times 9) + (6 \times 80) + (70 \times 9) + (70 \times 80) = 54 + 480 + 630 + 5,600$. Once this conceptual understanding is developed, they compare the problems in the algorithm with the component parts in the equation. (Figure 6.1 shows these rectangles within the larger array of 76×89.) In contrast, 70 percent of American teachers teach the algorithm as a series of procedures and interpret children's errors as a problem with carrying and lining up. They remind children of the "rules," that they are multiplying by tens and therefore have to move their answer to the next column. To help children follow the "rules" correctly, they often use lined paper and suggest that children use zero as a place holder.

FIGURE 6.1
An Array of the Algorithm

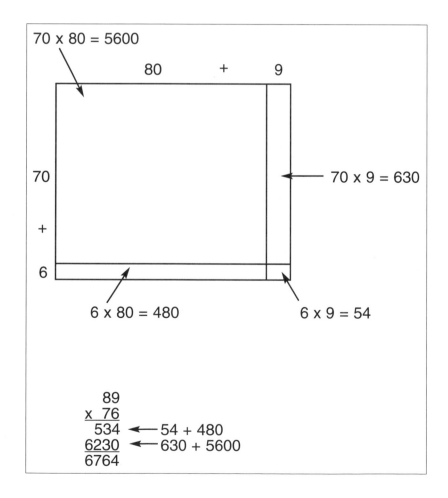

When children are invited to invent their own ways to decompose the problem—when they have not been taught the algorithm—they most often employ a form of the distributive property! Kamii (1993) found that when she asked children to solve double-digit multiplication problems like 76 × 89, most children began with the largest component. For example, they would break 76 × 89 up into 70 × 80 and 6 × 80, then add the remaining 70 × 9 and 6 × 9. The algorithm, though, requires starting with the units—therefore they had to give up their own meaning making just as they were constructing the distributive property in order to adopt the teacher's procedures.

Let's listen in as Sophie, a third grader, tries to make sense of the algorithm in a discussion with Willem Uittenbogaard. They are talking about packs of candy lifesavers that are packaged ten to a pack.

"How many lifesavers would you have if you had three packs, or five packs, or seven packs, or ten packs, or eleven packs?" Willem asks. Sophie easily multiplies by ten each time. Together they make a table to show the results. "What if the packs had eleven candies?"

Once again, Sophie begins to respond quickly. "In three packs there would be thirty-three; in five packs, fifty-five; in seven, seventy-seven; in ten, one hundred and ten." But then she pauses. "In eleven . . . I'm not sure. I need paper and pencil." She writes 11 × 11 in column fashion and attempts to perform the algorithm, but she makes a place value error:

```
  11
× 11
  11
  11
  22
```

Looking at her answer of 22, she says, "That can't be."

Willem says, "You already know ten packs is a hundred and ten."

Sophie nods, but does not use this information. She writes 11 eleven times in column fashion, then adds this long column to produce 121.

Willem confirms her answer and asks, "What about in twelve packs?"

Once again Sophie asks for paper and pencil and writes:

```
  11
× 12
  22
  11
  33
```

"Can't be." Again puzzled, she returns to her long column addition and adds another 11 on top. This time, however, she does not add each column but crosses out the 121 and writes down 132, obviously adding 11 to 121 in her head.

Sophie understands that this situation calls for multiplication. She understands that it can be solved by repeated addition. She knows that ten packs are 110 candies. She can multiply by ten easily. She demonstrates that she is aware of the distributive property when she adds one more 11 to 121 (which she even does mentally). She also has a good enough sense of number to know that her answers of 22 and 33 can't be right. Her problem is that the algorithm is getting in the way of her sense making. She treats the numeral 1 in 12 as a unit rather than a ten. She is performing a series of memorized steps, rather than trusting in her own mathematical sense.

One could argue that if we taught the algorithm conceptually rather than procedurally, more understanding would result. That is probably true. One could, in fact, build a bridge from children's invented solutions to the algorithm using the distributive property and rectangular arrays. With Sophie, Willem could write out $12 \times 11 = (2 \times 1) + (2 \times 10) + (10 \times 1) + (10 \times 10)$, build an array, and then look at the pieces of the algorithm with her, picking them out within the larger 12×11 array. But in today's world, do we want Sophie to have to rely on paper and pencil, or do we want to help her trust in her own mathematical sense and add another 11 to 110? She can do this in her head. Is the algorithm the fastest, most efficient, way to compute? When are algorithms helpful? What does it mean to compute with number sense? How would a mathematician solve 76×89?

Ann Dowker (1992) asked forty-four mathematicians to do several typical multiplication and division computation problems, one of which was 76×89, and assessed their strategies. Only 4 percent of the responses, across all the problems and across all mathematicians, were solved with algorithms. The mathematicians looked at the numbers first, then found efficient strategies that fit the numbers well. They made the numbers friendly and they played with relationships. Interestingly, they also varied their strategies, sometimes using different strategies for the same problems when they were asked about them on different days! They appeared to pick a strategy that seemed appropriate to the numbers and that was prevalent in their minds at that time; they searched for efficiency and elegance of solution; they made numbers friendly (often by using landmark numbers); and they found the process creative and enjoyable. A common strategy for 76×89 was: $(100 \times 76) - (11 \times 76) = 7,600 - 760 - 76 = 6,764$ (see the rectangular array in Figure 6.2). The commutative and distributive properties were employed to make the problem "friendlier."

There are many other ways to do this problem. Halving helps. If $100 \times 89 = 8,900$, then half of that equals 4,450, which is therefore equal to 50×89. To find 25×89, we take half of 4,450; that equals 2,225. Adding these together, we get $4,450 + 2,225 = 6,675 = 75 \times 89$. Now we just need to add one more 89 to get an answer of 6,764. (See the array in Figure 6.3.)

Using fractions is even nicer. Seventy-six is close to 75, which is three-fourths of a dollar. Three-fourths of $89 = 3 \times 22\frac{1}{4} = 66\frac{3}{4}$. Since we divided

75 by 100 to get the original three-fourths, we now have to multiply 66¾ by 100, which equals 6,675, the answer to 75 × 89. Now we need one more 89 to make 76 × 89: 6,675 + 89 = 6,764.

Or we could make the problem friendlier by first working with landmark numbers. Eighty times 90 = 7,200, then subtract 4 × 90. We now

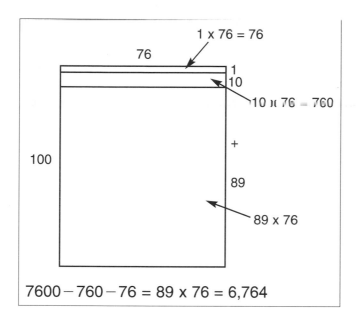

FIGURE 6.2
*A Common
Mathematician's
Strategy*

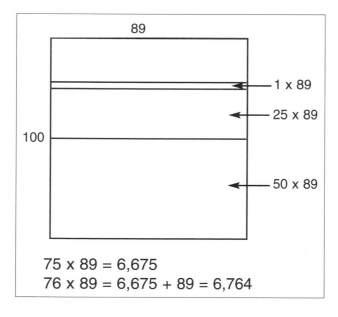

FIGURE 6.3
A Halving Strategy

have 76 × 90 = 6,840. To get to 76 × 89 we need to subtract one more row of 76. Thus, the final answer is 6,764. (See Figure 6.4.)

Note how all of these alternative, creative ways have far fewer steps than the algorithm and can be done more quickly. Some can be done mentally, others may require paper and pencil to keep track. Playing with numbers like this is based on a deep understanding of number, landmark numbers, and operations, and it characterizes true number sense.

Algorithms can nevertheless be helpful, particularly when multiplying or dividing large, nonfriendly numbers of four, five, or six digits. But for most two-digit problems, whatever the numbers, the algorithm is slower. It only seems faster to most adults because they have always used algorithms and have practiced them for many, many years. The procedures have become habits that require little thinking.

FIGURE 6.4
Using Landmarks

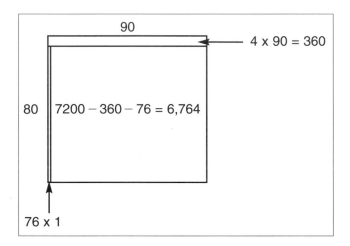

THE HISTORY OF ALGORITHMS

Through time and across cultures many different algorithms have been used for multiplication. For example, for many years Egyptians used an algorithm based on doubling. To multiply 28 × 12 (or 12 × 28), they would calculate 1 × 28 = 28, 2 × 28 = 56, 4 × 28 = 112, 8 × 28 = 224, and so on. As soon as they had parts that added up to 12, they would stop doubling and add these parts: 8 + 4 = 12, therefore 112 and 224 added together (336) equals 12 × 28.

Russian peasants used a halving and doubling algorithm. To multiply 28 × 12, they would first halve the 28 and double the 12, getting 14 × 24. Next they would repeat the procedure, getting 7 × 48. If an odd number (like 7 in this case) appeared, resulting in a remainder when halved, they would round down: 3 (instead of 3½) × 96, 1 (instead of 1½) × 192. They continued halving and doubling until they reached the last problem in the series (1 × *n*), in this case 1 × 192. Then they added up all the factors with odd multipliers—48 + 96 + 192 in this case—and arrived at the answer—28 × 12 = 336.

The algorithms for multiplication and division that we teach in most schools today were invented by the great Arab mathematician Muhammad ibn Musa al-Khwarizmi in the early part of the ninth century as an efficient computation strategy to replace the abacus. (In Latin his name was Algorismus—hence the term *algorithm*.) During this time, calculations using large numbers were needed both in the marketplace and for merchants' accounting purposes. Because calculations on the abacus were actions, there was no written record of the arithmetic, only the answer. And only the intelligentsia, practiced in the art of the abacus, could calculate. Denis Guedj (1996) describes a bit of the history:

> In the Middle Ages computations were carried out on an abacus, also called a computing table, a calculating device resembling a table with columns or ruled horizontal lines; digits were represented by counters, or apices. From the twelfth century on, this type of abacus was progressively replaced by the dust board as a tool of calculations. This development did not come about without a struggle between those who, evoking the ancient Greek mathematician Pythagoras, championed the abacus and those who became masters of algorism, the new Arabic number system. In this competition between the Ancients and Moderns, the former saw themselves as the keepers of the secrets of the art of computation and the defenders of the privileges of the guild of professional calculators . . . [while] the new system indisputably marked the democratization of computation. (53–54)

With the invention of the algorithms, and the dissemination of multiplication tables to use while performing them, even the most complex computations were possible, and written records of the calculations could be kept.

Schools soon set about to teach the procedures. In the Renaissance in Europe the manipulation of numbers and the practice of arithmetic were signs of advanced learning; those who knew how to multiply and divide with algorithms were guaranteed a professional career. In the Musée de Cluny, in Paris, there is a sixteenth-century tapestry depicting Lady Arithmetic teaching the new calculation methods to gilded youth. (A photograph of this is used as the lead photo in this chapter.)

But today's world is different. Human beings have continued through the centuries to design and build tools with which to calculate: from the slide rule, in 1621; to the first mechanical calculator, invented by Pascal in 1642; to the handheld calculator, in 1967; to today's graphic calculators. The World Wide Web even provides virtual calculators (Guedj 1996). Difficult computations, originally solved by algorithms, are now done with these tools.

Does this mean we don't need to know how to calculate? Of course not. But to be successful in today's world, we also need a deep conceptual understanding of mathematics. We are bombarded with numbers, statistics, advertisements, and similar data every day—on the radio, on television, and in newspapers. We need good mental ability and good number sense in order to evaluate advertising claims, estimate quantities, calculate efficiently the numbers we deal with every day and judge whether these calculations are reasonable, add up restaurant checks and determine equal shares, interpret data and statistics, and so on.

TEACHING FOR NUMBER SENSE

Each day at the start of math workshop, Peter Markowitz, a fifth-grade teacher in East Harlem, New York, does a short minilesson on computation strategies. He usually chooses five or six related problems and asks the children to solve them and share their strategies with one another. Crucial to his choice of problems is the relationship between them. He picks problems that are likely to lead to a discussion of a specific strategy. He allows his students to construct their own strategies by decomposing numbers in ways that make sense to them. Posted around the room are signs the children have made throughout the year as they have developed a repertoire of strategies for multiplication. One reads "Keep on Doubling!"; another, "Friends of Ten"; a third, "Halves & Doubles" (see Figure 6.5). On the chalkboard is the string of problems the children are discussing.

Taniqua is describing how she used a halving and doubling strategy to solve 50 × 14. "I cut the fourteen in half and doubled the fifty to make the problem one hundred times seven," she explains. "It's like half of a hundred times fourteen, which is fourteen hundred. So it has to be seven hundred."

Dominick agrees with her but has a different way as well. "You could also do ten times fifty, plus four times fifty," he explains. "That's easy, too. You just have to add five hundred and two hundred."

Nathan raises his hand, and Peter asks him to explain his method. Nathan's way is not as efficient, but it makes sense to him: "I knew that ten times fourteen was one hundred and forty, and I needed five times that, so I added it up."

Peter writes 140 + 140 + 140 + 140 + 140 = 700, and comments, "That's a lot of steps. But it's certainly better than writing fourteen fifty times, isn't it? Which way do you think is the most efficient of all the ways offered so far?" Most of the children agree that Taniqua's and Dominick's ways are more efficient.

Natalie suggests a shortcut to Nathan. "You could do twenty times fourteen twice. That's two hundred and eighty plus two hundred and eighty."

"How many fourteens is that?" Peter asks, not sure whether Natalie thinks she has completed the problem.

"Forty," she replies.

"So, Nathan, what do we have to do next?" Peter asks.

Nathan pauses, at first not sure. But then he offers, "Ten. So that's a hundred and forty more."

"Do we have fifty times fourteen now?" Peter probes. Nathan is confident, so Peter continues, "There are lots of different ways to break the problem up . . . so whatever comes to you, use that. Let's try another." Peter writes 24 × 14 next, directly underneath 50 × 14.

"I used twenty times fourteen." Juan starts the discussion, explaining how the prior problem helped. "I knew that was 280, so I just added four more fourteens. That was fifty-six."

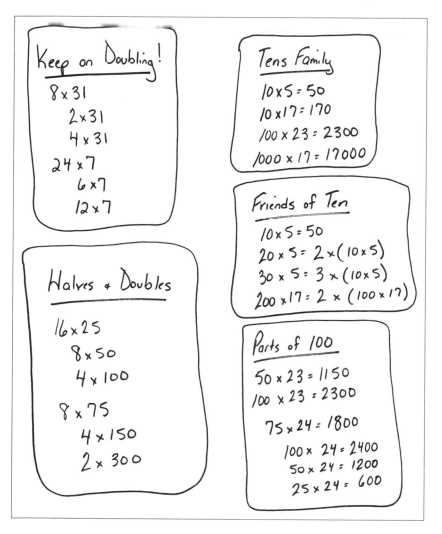

FIGURE 6.5 *Signs Made by the Children in Peter's Class*

Abraham offers a halving strategy, also using the prior problem. "I knew that fifty times fourteen was seven hundred, so twenty-five times fourteen is half of that, or 350. Then I just subtracted a fourteen."

Peter asks a couple of children to paraphrase what Abraham did to see whether they understand. Then he asks, "And why did he subtract?" Everyone seems clear that it is to achieve 24 × 14, one group of 14 less than 25 × 14. "So why do you think Juan used twenty-five? What makes twenty-five so nice?"

Several children say, "Money."

"Yes, it's like money, a quarter. Bobby?"

"And it's part of one hundred."

"Yes, it's a real nice part of one hundred, isn't it. Halving the fifty made it nice."

Peter goes on with his string using other numbers around fifty— 48 × 7 and then 51 × 23.

For 48 × 7, Bobby doubles and halves. "It's the same as twenty-four times fourteen," he explains, "I split the fourteen in half and doubled the twenty-four."

"Wow. Done!" Peter is impressed. "You didn't need to calculate at all! What if twenty-four times fourteen hadn't been solved already? Is there any other way? Dominick?"

Dominick uses fifty. "I knew a hundred times seven was seven hundred, so fifty times seven is 350. Then I subtracted two sevens, or fourteen."

These young mathematicians are composing and decomposing flexibly as they calculate multiplication problems. They are inventing their own strategies. They are looking for relationships between the problems. They are looking at the numbers first before they decide on a strategy.

Children don't do this automatically. Peter has developed this ability in his students by focusing on computation during minilessons with strings of related problems every day. He has developed the big ideas and models through investigations. But once this understanding has been constructed, he hones computation strategies in minilessons.

Traditionally, mathematics educators thought teaching for number sense meant helping children connect their actions to real objects. We used base ten blocks and trading activities to help children understand regrouping. We built arrays with base ten materials and looked at the dimensions and the area. We bundled straws, popsicle sticks, or other units into tens and hundreds, trying to develop a connection for children between the actions of regrouping the objects and the symbolic notation in the algorithms. We talked about the connection between the concrete, the pictorial, and the symbolic. But all of these pedagogical techniques were used to teach the algorithms. The goal of arithmetic teaching was algorithms, albeit with understanding.

In the 1980s, educators began to discuss whether the goal of arithmetic computation should be algorithms at all. Constance Kamii's research has led her to insist that teaching algorithms is in fact harmful to children's mathematical development (Kamii and Dominick 1998). First, she examined children's invented procedures for multiplication and division and found that children's procedures for multiplication always went from left to right, from the largest units to the smallest. With division, children's procedures went from the smallest units to the largest, from right to left. Yet the algorithms require opposite procedures: with multiplication one starts with the units and works right to left; with division, one starts with the largest unit (hundreds, for example) and works right to left. Children necessarily had to give up their own meaning making in order to perform the algorithms. The algorithms hindered children's ability to construct an understanding of the distributive property of multiplication and of place value, making them dependent on the spatial arrangement of digits on paper. They required that children see themselves as proficient users of someone else's mathematics, not as mathematicians.

Kamii's data, and her strong arguments from a developmental perspective, are convincing, and many educators have begun to allow children to construct their own computation strategies. This isn't enough, however. Although their invented strategies do become more efficient over time, these strategies are remarkably similar—most are based on some form of the distributive property and on breaking the number into place value components—and many of them are cumbersome and inefficient.

Over the last seven years or so Mathematics in the City has looked seriously at how to develop in students a repertoire of efficient computation strategies that are based on a deep understanding of number sense and operation and that honor children's own constructions. The next chapter describes the techniques we have been using and the strategies we try to develop for multiplication and division.

SUMMING UP . . .

Algorithms were developed in the Middle Ages by the Arab mathematician al-Khwarizmi. The use of algorithms brought about a democratization of computation; people no longer had to rely on the select few who were competent users of the abacus. When algorithms appeared, there was political tension between those who wanted to hold on to the abacus and those who wanted to learn the new methods. Interestingly, a similar political situation exists today. As schools have begun to reform their teaching, as algorithms have been replaced with mental math strategies and calculating with number sense, arguments have broken out between those who fight to maintain the "old" math and those who favor reform. Many newspaper articles play into the fear that children will not be able to compute. This fear is based on uninformed, often mistaken, notions of the reform. Parents are products of the old education, and therefore they define mathematics as the skills they were taught. When they don't see their children learning what they believe to be the goals of mathematics—the algorithms—they assume that nothing is being learned. Many of them have called the new mathematics "fuzzy" or "soft" and described it as a "dumbing down."

Algorithms—a structured series of procedures that can be used across problems, regardless of the numbers—do have an important place in mathematics. After students have a deep understanding of number relationships and operations and have developed a repertoire of computation strategies, they may find it interesting to investigate why the traditional computation algorithms work. Exploring strategies that can be used with larger, messy numbers when a calculator is not handy is an interesting inquiry—one in which the traditional algorithms can be employed. In these inquiries algorithms can surface as a formal, generalized procedure. An alternative approach when the numbers are not nice. Often algorithms come up in classroom discussions, too, because parents have taught them to their children and children attempt to use them without understanding why they work. Exploring them and figuring out why they work may deepen children's understanding.

Algorithms should not be the primary goal of computation instruction, however. Using algorithms, the same series of steps with all problems, is antithetical to calculating with number sense. Calculating with number sense means that one should look at the numbers first and then decide on a strategy that is fitting—and efficient. Developing number sense takes time; algorithms taught too early work against the development of good number sense. Children who learn to think, rather than to apply the same procedures by rote regardless of the numbers, will be empowered. They will not see mathematics as a dogmatic, dead discipline, but as a living, creative one. They will thrive on inventing their own rules, because these rules will serve afterward as the foundation for solving other problems.

By abandoning the rote teaching of algorithms, we are not asking children to learn less, we are asking them to learn more. We are asking them to mathematize, to think like mathematicians, to look at the numbers before they calculate. To paraphrase Plato, we are asking children to approach mathematics as free men. Children can and do construct their own strategies, and when they are allowed to make sense of calculations in their own ways, they understand better. In the words of the mathematician Blaise Pascal, "We are usually convinced more easily by reasons we have found ourselves than by those which have occurred to others."

In focusing on number sense, we are also asking teachers to think mathematically. We are asking them to develop their own mental math strategies in order to develop them in their students. Once again teachers are on the edge, not only the edge between the structure and development of mathematics, but also the edge between the old and the new—between the expectations of parents and the expectations of the new tests and the new curricula.

The backlash is strong, and walking this edge is difficult. Teachers need support. Learning to teach in a way that supports mathematizing—in a way that supports calculating with number sense—takes time. Sometimes, parents have responded by hiring tutors to teach their children the algo-rithms—a solution that has often been detrimental to children as they grapple to understand number and operation. Sometimes, as teachers have attempted to reform their practice, children have been left with no algorithms and no repertoire of strategies, only their own informal, inefficient inven-tions. The reform will fail if we do not approach calculation seriously, if we do not produce children who can calculate efficiently. Parents will define our success in terms of the their old notions of mathematics. They saw the goal of arithmetic, of school mathematics, as calculation. They will look for what they know, for what they learned, for what they define as mathematics.

7 | DEVELOPING EFFICIENT COMPUTATION WITH MINILESSONS

*I think, therefore I am. . . . Each problem that I solved
became a rule which served afterwards to solve other
problems.*
—René Descartes

*Mathematics is the only instructional material that
can be presented in an entirely undogmatic way.*
—Max Dehn

MINILESSONS WITH MENTAL MATH STRINGS

"I knew that six times six was thirty-six, so I took away six. That gave me
thirty." Diana, a New York City fourth grader, is explaining how she solved
the problem 5×6. Her friend Linda, who is sitting next to her, agrees with
this answer but shares a different strategy. "I knew ten times six was sixty,
so half of that is thirty." Most of the other children know the fact by heart,
and Grady Carson, their teacher, continues with his string of problems. He
writes 30×6 next. Randy explains that he added 30 and 30 to get 60. Then
he added 60 three times to get 180.

Grady is beginning math workshop, as he normally does each day, with
a short ten- or fifteen-minute minilesson focusing on computation strategies. In contrast to investigations, which characterize the heart of math
workshop, the minilessons are more guided and more explicit. They are
designed specifically to highlight certain strategies and to develop efficient mental math computation. Each day, Grady chooses a string of four
or five related problems and asks his students to solve them. Together they
discuss and compare strategy efficiency and explore relationships between
problems.

Crucial to Grady's choice of problems is the relationship between them.
He picks problems that are likely to develop certain strategies or big ideas
that he knows are important because they are landmarks on the landscape
of learning. We call these groups of problems *strings* because they are a
structured series of computation problems that are related in such a way as

to develop and highlight number relationships and operations. Designing such strings and other minilessons to develop computation strategies requires that teachers have a <u>repertoire</u> of strategies for multiplication and division and that they know how to <u>play</u> with numbers.

Choosing the Strategies, Choosing the Numbers

The string that Grady is using is shown in Figure 7.1. Grady has chosen these numbers to encourage children to use the distributive property, which is the basis for why the traditional multiplication algorithm works. When we multiply 12 × 13 using the algorithm, we are actually multiplying first by 2 and then by ten—2 × (3 + 10) + 10 × (3 + 10). The twelve groups can be broken up into different parts, each part multiplied by 13. As long as all twelve groups of thirteen are accounted for, the sum of the answers to the parts will be the answer to the whole: (6 × 13) + (6 × 13) = 12 × 13; (4 × 13) + (8 × 13) = 12 × 13. When children are just taught the procedures of the algorithm, which require them to treat each number as a digit regardless of its quantity, they lose sight of the arrays they are dealing with and an understanding of the distributive property is often sacrificed. (Remember how Sophie [in Chapter 6] could not multiply 11 × 11 with the algorithm but knew 10 × 11 and 1 × 11?)

Grady wants to develop children's ability to use the distributive property with understanding. He does this by using a string of problems that will

FIGURE 7.1
Grady's String

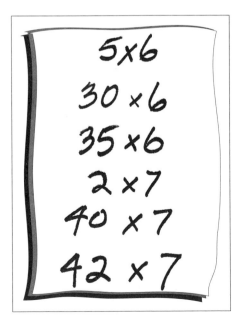

bring the distributive property to the surface for discussion. Note the relationships in Grady's string. The answers to the first two problems when added produce the third. The next three problems are similarly related.

Although Grady has thought about the problems beforehand and has a string of related problems ready, he does not put all the problems on the board at once. Instead he writes one at a time, and children discuss their strategies before the subsequent problem is presented. This way, the children can consider the strategies from the prior problem as well as the numbers, and they are prompted to think about the relationships of the problems in the string as they go along. Sometimes, depending on the strategies he hears, Grady adjusts the problems in his planned string on the spot to ensure that the strategies he is attempting to develop are discussed and tried out. Let's witness this in action.

Grady continues with 35 × 6. "Becky?"

"I added thirty-five six times," Becky explains. "But to make it easier I added thirty-five and thirty-five to get seventy, like Randy did before. Then I doubled seventy and added another. That gave me 210."

Steve nods his head in agreement but continues with a smile, "I have a shorter way. The last two problems add up to the answer!"

Grady asks him to explain.

"I split thirty-five into thirty and five, and I did thirty times six first. Then I did five times six, and I added them together."

Grady draws the open array shown in Figure 7.2 to represent Steve's steps and help the other children visualize the parts. "That's pretty neat, isn't it? Who can explain his strategy? Diana?"

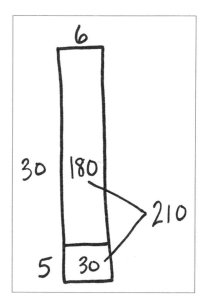

FIGURE 7.2
Steve's Strategy for
35 × 6

"He broke thirty-five up into two parts, thirty and five, then he multiplied each piece," Diana says, quite succinctly.

Surprised that the pattern has been noticed so quickly, Grady skips the next two problems in his string and goes immediately to 42 × 7. He wants to see whether the children can find the component parts themselves. "Can we use Steve's strategy for this one?"

Robert offers an answer of 280, and Grady asks him to explain what he did.

"I knew four times seven was twenty-eight, so forty times seven is 280." Robert has used the associative property for this part of his solution, but now he looks puzzled. "Uh. . . ."

Grady draws the open array for 40 × 7 and labels it 280. "What did you leave out?"

"Oh. yeah, two times seven."

Grady completes the open array (see Figure 7.3). "This is such a neat strategy that you came up with, Steve. How about if we make a sign to post with our other strategies. Steve, how can we phrase it?"

"Split the two-digit number into tens and ones," Steve offers as the first step. "And then multiply each number by the other number."

"What do we think of that?" Grady throws the description back to the class to ponder.

"How about if we say 'factor' for 'the other number'?" suggests Diana.

"Oh, nice," Grady says. "I love it when you use specific mathematical language."

FIGURE 7.3
*Robert's Strategy for
42 × 7*

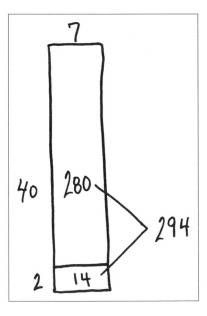

Although Grady had not intended to focus on writing a description of the strategy, mathematics is also involved in this process. As children grapple with language that is specific, that clearly communicates what they want to say, they come to appreciate the need for mathematical language. They grapple with definitions and mathematical terms.

"Let's use the word *factor* again," Grady suggests. "How about, 'split one factor into tens and units and multiply each part by the other factor'? And then what is the answer called?"

Several children chorus, "The product," and Grady adds, "That gives you the product." The sign now reads, "Split one factor into tens and ones and multiply each part by the other factor. That gives you the product." Grady posts it with other signs listing strategies discussed in earlier minilessons.

Just because one child has constructed a strategy does not mean all the other children in the class understand it and can use it meaningfully. Posted signs have the danger of becoming a list of algorithms that children will adopt as rote procedures. Grady wants to ensure that his students understand the strategies dealt with in his minilessons. Therefore, he concludes this minilesson with three more problems (25 × 9; 26 × 9; 46 × 5) and suggests that the children try them using Steve's strategy, recording the problems in their journals, drawing arrays, and then sharing their work with a partner.

Tools, Representations, and Models

By asking the children to draw arrays as they try out Steve's strategy, Grady has them model the problem. He used this same process when he drew an array for 40 × 7 for Robert. The piece missing, 2 × 7, became apparent. Of course, for this modeling to help, children need to understand that the array comprises rows and columns. Tools such as square tiles and graph paper, employed while investigating contexts like those described in previous chapters, are essential to help children develop an understanding of arrays. Grady's students have already investigated many arraylike contexts.

Here, as Grady's students represent their strategies on paper, they are able to check out whether they have done all the parts. They are using the array as a model to think with—as a tool. Understanding the distributive property is a big idea. Often children confuse the factors they have done and the factors they still need to do. The part/whole relationships can be difficult to keep track of mentally. Two of Grady's students have just this struggle as they discuss solving to 26 × 9 based on their solution to 25 × 9.

"You just add one more."

"But one more what? A twenty-five or a nine?"

"Twenty-five. The answer's 250."

"No, I don't think so. Twenty-five times nine is twenty-five nines. We need twenty-six nines. So we need one more nine." They finally succeed in drawing the arrays shown in Figure 7.4. "See, when you added twenty-five, that was twenty-five times ten."

"Oh, yeah. Boy, this is confusing, isn't it?"

While doing strings, Grady (like Miki in Chapter 5) has used the open array as a model to *represent* children's strategies. This visible representation focuses discussion. Over time, children move from using the graph paper array as a tool, to using an open array to represent their thinking, to mentally using an array as a model for thinking.

FIGURE 7.4
*Children's work
25 × 10 versus 26 × 9*

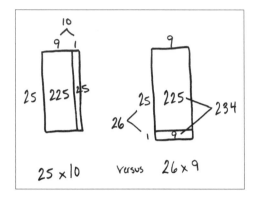

DEVELOPING MULTIPLICATION AND DIVISION STRATEGIES

Extending the Distributive Property

The distributive property can also be used in connection with subtraction. For example, 49 × 7 can be solved as (50 × 7) − 7. Peter Markowitz's fifth graders named this strategy "friends, more or less"—meaning they could use a friendly number, like 50 or 100, and then add or subtract as needed. Let's watch this strategy in action.

Peter writes 48 × 7 on the board. "Treshaun?"

Treshaun makes use of fifty. "I knew one hundred times seven was 700, so fifty times seven is 350. Then I subtracted fourteen."

"And for ninety-eight times thirty-two??

"That's one hundred times thirty-two minus sixty-four. Friends, more or less." (See the array in Figure 7.5.)

The distributive property can also be used when the numbers can't be made friendly so easily. Peter's fifth graders call this strategy "the ugly one," because it has so many parts. For example, 37 × 84 might be solved as (30 × 80) + (7 × 80) + (30 × 4) + (7 × 4)—see the array in Figure 7.6.

Using the Associative Property

Understanding that the order in which the factors are multiplied doesn't affect the result is a big idea for children and must be constructed through investigations such as the Christmas ornaments investigation Hollee Freeman uses in Chapter 3. Even after children understand this idea, though, they do not automatically use it when computing. Mental math strings can be used to help children develop computational strategies based on this idea. Let's return to Grady Carson's class on another day.

Grady begins his minilesson with the problem 10 × 6 = ?. All the students are clustered around him, math journals in hand. Grady assumes no one will have trouble solving this problem, and he will use it as the basis for the strategy he is trying to develop. He calls on Caroline and is not surprised by her answer.

"Sixty," Caroline responds quickly. "I just know that one."

Other children nod in agreement, and Grady continues with his string, writing 3 × 6 underneath 10 × 6 = 60. Once again, this is easy. Several children respond, "Eighteen."

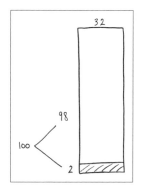

FIGURE 7.5
Friends More or Less
98 × 32 = (100 × 32) −
(2 × 32)

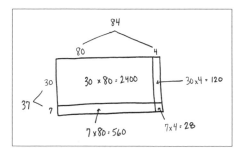

FIGURE 7.6
Array for 37 × 84
The Ugly One

Grady adds 18 as the product and adds a third problem to the board, 30 × 6. The children can't solve this problem as readily. They take more time to figure it out. Grady waits a bit, then asks for solutions and strategies. "Randy?"

"One hundred and eighty."

"How did you do it?" Grady inquires.

"I added ten times six, which was sixty, three times."

Grady draws the open array in Figure 7.7 and writes 3 × (6 × 10) underneath.

John comments, "It's also three times six is eighteen, so just add a zero for thirty times six."

"Did you add a zero to eighteen? Is three plus zero thirty?"

John looks puzzled but shakes his head. "No. I just put the zero on the end. I didn't really add it."

"So that's a pattern you've noticed," Grady acknowledges and writes (3 × 6) × 10.

"Let's try another." Grady writes 4 × 7.

"Twenty-four . . . no, twenty-eight," responds Robert. "Two times seven is fourteen, so I doubled it."

Grady adds the answer and writes 10 × 7. Again, this is easy, and Grady writes in the 70. He follows with 40 × 7 to ensure that the pattern resulting from the associative property—4 × (7 × 10) = (4 × 7) × 10—will appear.

Several children immediately use the pattern. "Two hundred and eighty. It's four times seven with a zero on the end."

"We've been using a pattern that John and several others noticed as we worked through this string," Grady summarizes. "But, of course, to be sure it will always work, we have to figure out why it is happening. For homework, draw some arrays. See if you can figure out why it is happening. Why is it, if you are multiplying, say, sixty times eight, you can do it by multiplying six times eight and putting a zero on the end?"

In this minilesson Grady is highlighting the associative property. He has done this by choosing problems whose answers are similarly patterned. Although his fourth graders can now solve problems like 40 × 7 easily, they

FIGURE 7.7
Randy's Strategy

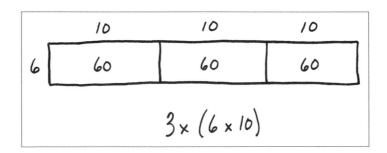

may or may not fully understand why it works to multiply $(4 \times 7) \times 10$. However, as they investigate this strategy in their journals, Grady will be able to analyze their thinking about this topic and respond to it. The information he gleans will help him determine what to do next as he helps his students move through the landscape of learning.

Doubling and Halving

This strategy is directly connected to the associative property, but because it is so important, we are highlighting it separately. As we describe in Chapter 3, children begin to use doubling early on. To figure out 4×7, for example, they do 2×7 and double it. Making use of landmark numbers and then doubling or halving is a powerful strategy for double-digit computation as well. To calculate 4×35, we might double 70; to calculate 50×42, we might take half of 4,200 (see Figure 7.8). Developing these strategies using problems strings and open arrays is easy. As long as the problems make use of this pattern, the arrays simply get cut in half or doubled. A sample string for developing these strategies is 2×24, 4×24, 8×24, 8×12, 4×12, and so on.

The strategy becomes even more powerful when doubling and halving are used simultaneously. For example, $3\frac{1}{2} \times 14$ can easily be solved by doubling the $3\frac{1}{2}$ and halving the 14: 7×7. The array in Figure 7.9 shows why this strategy works. It is based on the associative property, because the doubling and halving is a result of how one associates the factors— $3\frac{1}{2} \times (2 \times 7) = (3\frac{1}{2} \times 2) \times 7$. Once children understand what happens to the product when one factor is doubled *or* halved, the string can be expanded to include problems where doubling *and* halving are used simultaneously. A slight variation on the string above brings this relationship to the surface: 2×24, 4×24, 2×48, 8×12, 16×6, 32×3, and so on.

This strategy can be generalized to any number and its reciprocal: 3, $\frac{1}{3}$; 10, $\frac{1}{10}$; and so on. A messy problem like $18 \times 3\frac{1}{3}$ can be solved by taking a third of eighteen, and multiplying three and a third by three. This results in 6×10, an easy problem to solve. Similarly, $.8 \times 30$ can be solved by 8×3. Strings can bring these patterns to the surface, and children can then investigate why the strategy works by drawing arrays on graph paper.

Using Money

Because money is such a powerful and ever present context in children's lives, it can be used to develop landmark numbers like 25, 50, and 75. Let's listen as Carol Mosesson's third graders discuss their multiplication strategies based on the use of money. Zenique is sharing how he came up with 190 as the answer to 20×9.

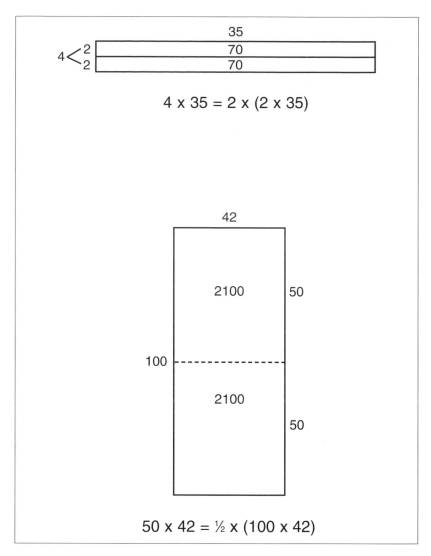

$$4 \times 35 = 2 \times (2 \times 35)$$

$$50 \times 42 = \tfrac{1}{2} \times (100 \times 42)$$

FIGURE 7.8

"Five twenty-dollar bills is a hundred dollars," he begins, "so another five is two hundred. Oh, I know what I did wrong. I only took away ten. I should have taken away a twenty-dollar bill. It is 180," he concludes, agreeing with an answer given by another classmate.

"Money is a clever way to think about that problem, Zenique." Carol writes 25 × 9 on the board. "How about this one? Shakira?"

"Three hundred . . . no, 225. I counted by twenty-five."

"How many twenty-fives would it take to make three hundred?" Carol probes.

Shakira answers quickly, "Twelve."

Carol is surprised. "Wow, how did you know that so fast?"

"I knew four quarters made a dollar, so times three, that's twelve."

"That's exactly how I did it," Olana joins in. "I got 225 because I knew that four times twenty-five was a hundred, because that's like four quarters. So another four times twenty-five is another dollar. And one more quarter is 225.

To develop this type of thinking, teachers can begin a minilesson using real coins, or pictures of coins, in an array. For example, if a 4 × 4 array of quarters is shown, many children will explain that they know that each row is a dollar. Because quarters are worth twenty-five cents the problem can then be written as 16 × 25 and strategies developed—16 × 25 = 4 × (4 × 25), for example. After several minilessons based on money, children are able to use it as a context, even when the numbers are bare, like in strings.

Using Fractions

Once children develop a sense of landmark fractions, like ½, ¼, and ¾, using them can also become a powerful strategy. For example, 75 × 80 can easily be solved by thinking of the problem as ¾ × 80. You only have to remember to compensate for the decimal in the answer (multiply 60 by 100, because you treated 75 as 75/100).

Minilessons can be designed to develop this ability. If the problems in the strings progress from fractions to decimals to whole numbers, children quickly see the resulting patterns. For example, a string like ¼ × 80, .25 × 80, 25 × 80, ½ × 60, .5 × 60, .50 × 60, 50 × 60 produces the appropriate patterns in the answers, and children can use arrays to explore the relationships.

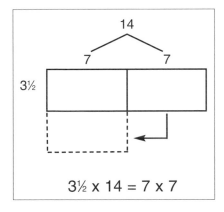

FIGURE 7.9

USING THE OPEN ARRAY WITH DIVISION

Division is defined, mathematically, as the inverse of multiplication. Traditionally, when teaching the long division algorithm, teachers have encouraged children to think about division as a "goes into" action. For example, seventy-five divided by five was taught as five goes into seven once, with two left over, which is joined with the five, and five then goes into twenty-five five times, for an answer of fifteen. Teaching division as a "goes into" action is an insufficient model, and treating digits separately is confusing and often makes little sense to children.

When children are allowed to construct their own division strategies, they often use multiplication, building up to the whole rather than subtracting from the whole. The open array represents both repeated addition and subtraction strategies well, and it develops the connection between multiplication and division. The pictures are the same for multiplication and division, but the knowns and unknowns are different (see Figure 7.10).

Reducing

Let's watch Andrea Franks use an open array with a division string to develop a reducing strategy with her fourth and fifth graders in New York City. Andrea has written 24/6 on the chalkboard.

"Four," Abbie, a fourth grader, states with confidence. "I just knew that one."

FIGURE 7.10

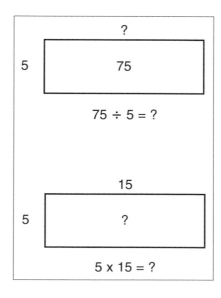

All Andrea's students know this fact by heart, so she moves on, writing 48/12 underneath it. "Sue?"

Again, this is an easy problem. "Four. I knew that twelve times two is twenty-four, so I doubled: twenty-four times two is forty-eight."

Andrea draws the open array shown in Figure 7.11 and asks other students to paraphrase what Sue did. Then, continuing her string, she writes 48/6. Children's answers vary. Some say two; others, eight. Interestingly, although most of the children know the multiplication fact 8 × 6, they are so intent on looking for relationships in the string they don't think about it right away. Andrea asks Anton, who has answered two, to explain.

"You cut the twelve from the last problem in half, so I halved the answer."

As is common as children try to apply the doubling and halving they have used in multiplication to division, Anton has halved the answer when he should have doubled it. Andrea draws an array of his thinking: the array remaining after halving twelve to six and halving four to two produces an area of only twelve, not forty-eight (see Figure 7.12).

Afrique, a fifth grader who has gotten eight as an answer, explains, "No, Anton, you need to move the right part of the array down, underneath the four-by-six array." Andrea draws the rearranged array (see Figure 7.13).

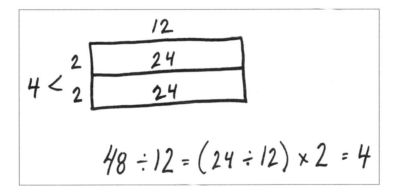

FIGURE 7.11
Sue's Strategy

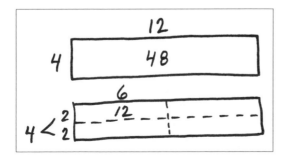

FIGURE 7.12
Anton's Strategy

Ray, who has gotten two as his answer, speaks up. "I don't get why you're moving that down, Afrique."

"Because you need it to be six, not twelve, but you still need the inside to be forty-eight." Afrique's reasoning convinces Ray, as well as the rest of the children.

Andrea goes on with her string, this time writing 96/12. After giving the students time to think out the relationship, she calls on Verona, one of her fourth graders.

"Eight," responds Verona. "Because forty-eight divided by twelve is four. Ninety-six divided by twelve is double, so it has to be eight." Andrea draws the open array shown in Figure 7.14.

Afrique volunteers a different way. "I used forty-eight over six," she explains, as Andrea represents her thinking by drawing the array shown in Figure 7.15. "But I doubled both, so the answer is the same. Eight."

"But didn't you double both, too, Verona?" asks Ray.

"No, because I didn't start with forty-eight over six. I started with forty-eight over twelve. Only the forty-eight doubled."

Andrea is aware that Ray and probably other students are still confused. She asks them to consider each of the arrays and to compare Verona's strategy with Afrique's. "How many columns? How many rows?"

Lena responds, "There's twelve columns and eight rows in both. And they both doubled the forty-eight."

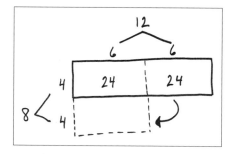

FIGURE 7.13
Afrique's Strategy

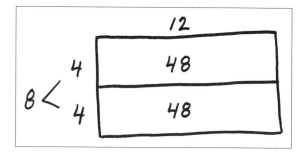

FIGURE 7.14
Verona's Strategy for 96/12

Ronnie, a fifth grader, interjects, "Hey, I just noticed this now. They both kind of doubled and doubled. Verona doubled the forty-eight and the four. Afrique doubled the forty-eight and the six."

Ronnie's insight is a "teachable moment"—an important moment to explore the connection between the doubling and halving strategy in multiplication and the reducing strategy in division. Andrea decides to focus discussion on this relationship. "Let's look at the multiplication problems for each of these division problems." She writes:

$$48/12 = 4$$
$$48/6 = 8$$
$$48/3 = 16$$
$$48/1.5 = 32$$

Then she asks the children for the multiplication problem related to each of these division problems and writes them down as well:

$48/12 = 4$	$4 \times 12 = 48$
$48/6 = 8$	$8 \times 6 = 48$
$48/3 = 16$	$16 \times 3 = 48$
$48/1.5 = 32$	$32 \times 1.5 = 48$

"What's happening in the division? What's happening in the multiplication?"

"Whew, I'm getting confused." Ray laughs.

"What's happening, Ray?" Andrea laughs too.

Ray attempts to explain. "For the answer to be the same in multiplication you had to double one number and halve the other. But with division, when the answers are the same, then both numbers have been doubled or halved."

"What about when only the divisor doubles?" Andrea probes.

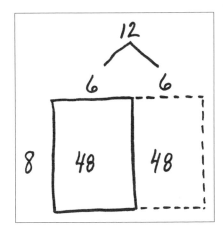

FIGURE 7.15
Afrique's Strategy
for 96/12

Ray ponders, beginning to make sense of the relationship. "The answer is half," he concludes.

"And when the divisor halves?"

"The answer doubles."

Even though Ray appears to be able to explain the relationships, his understanding is probably still shaky. Many of his classmates, also, need more work with these relationships. The relationships between multiplication and division, and those involved in reducing, doubling, and halving, are very difficult for children. Andrea will need to continue this work, both with problem strings and with investigations in which children can explore changing arrays. As children represent one another's thinking using the open array, they become clearer about the relationships, which on a concrete level, with whole numbers, form the basis for later algebraic reasoning.

Using the Distributive Property of Multiplication for Division

The traditional long division algorithm is based on the distributive property of multiplication. To divide 275 by 25 using the long division algorithm, one begins by seeing how many times 25 goes into 27. The 27 is of course 27 tens, so when we say 25 goes in once, we really mean ten times. Ten times 25 is 250. The 25 that remains, divided by 25, is 1. Thus the answer is 11. What we have really done is $(25 \times 10) + (25 \times 1) = 25 \times 11$.

When we use the distributive property, we don't always necessarily have to break up the numbers in place value columns. Only the long division algorithm requires that. We could just as easily break the 275 into 200 plus 75. Two hundred divided by 25 equals 8, and 75 divided by 25 equals 3; $3 + 8 = 11$. Even nicer is 300 divided by 25 minus 25 divided by 25, or $12 - 1 = 11$.

Strings that develop the use of this strategy characterize this relationship. For example, we might start with a piece of the array, 100/25. The second problem would be another piece, such as 75/25; the third, the total: 175/25. Examples of similar strings are 150/15, 30/15, 180/15; 180/6, 36/6, 216/6; 300/6, 30/6, 270/6. The corresponding arrays are similar to the multiplication arrays (see Figure 7.16).

Putting It Together

Children can get used to being provided with the connected pieces in problem strings. For this reason, it is also important to present only one problem and have children solve it in as many different ways as they can. In this next excerpt, Andrea does just that.

"Here's a tough problem." Andrea writes 1,224/24 on the chalkboard. "How can we make it friendly?"

The students work in their math journals, calculating and drawing arrays to explain their thinking. Zoe offers to begin. "I halved both numbers to make 612 over twelve," she begins. "Then I halved again to get 306 over six. That gave me fifty-one."

"I did that, too, Zoe," Caleb says, "but I got 151."

"Is 151 times six equal to 306?" Andrea asks, encouraging Caleb to think about whether his answer is reasonable.

"No," Caleb admits. "But what did I do wrong?"

"Well, explain what you did."

Often the most powerful teaching moments come about while exploring wrong answers. Learners' strategies are always representative of their mathematical ideas, in this case about how division works. As Andrea explores with Caleb what was wrong with his strategy, his confusion about the distributive property of multiplication and its connection to division comes to the surface.

"I broke the 306 over six into one hundred over two plus one hundred over two plus one hundred over two. Then I did six divided by six, and that was one," Caleb explains, still puzzled about why this strategy didn't work.

Andrea draws a partial array of what Caleb has done (see Figure 7.17). "So what did you divide the three hundred by when you were done?" Andrea asks him to reflect on the array.

"Oh . . . only two." Caleb thinks some more. "I could do . . . let's see . . . three divided by six is one half. So three hundred divided by three is one hundred, so three hundred divided by six is fifty . . . oh, yeah. Fifty-one." Caleb has resolved his disequilibrium.

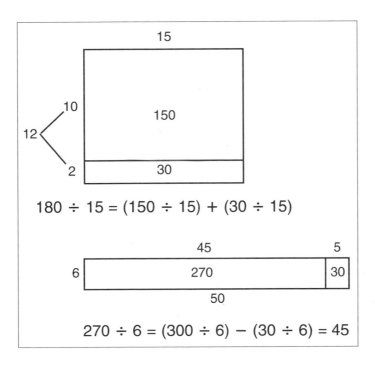

FIGURE 7.16

Andrea gives Caleb and the rest of the class a few moments to reflect and then moves on. "Any other ways? Verona?"

"I made the problem friendly by turning it into twelve hundred divided by twenty-four," she explains. "I knew that was fifty, because twelve hundred divided by twelve is one hundred. There's twenty-four left to be divided by twenty-four, so the answer is fifty-one."

"Wow, that's effective, isn't it?" Andrea points up the efficiency of Verona's solution. "Your way is kind of similar, isn't it, Ron?"

Ron nods. "But I doubled. I made the problem 2,448 divided by twenty-four. I knew that answer was 102, because twenty-four hundred divided by twenty-four is one hundred, and forty-eight divided by twenty-four is two. Then I halved the answer and I got fifty-one."

"Neat. Any other ways?"

Lena jumps in. "I did it like Zoe, but I just kept going with the halving to 153 divided by three. Then I did 150 divided by three plus three divided by three."

Andrea's students are flexibly composing and decomposing number just as the mathematicians did in Ann Dowker's research study (see Chapter 6). Their constructions are also reminiscent of the Egyptian and Russian multiplication algorithms based on doubling and halving. Had these children been restricted to the long division algorithm, the first step would have been to see how many times 24 fits into 122! Not only is the value of the whole number lost, but the division is harder. And where is the creativity? Instead, they are playing with number, taking risks, constructing at the edge of their knowledge, and enjoying the aesthetics of mathematics.

FIGURE 7.17
First Step of Caleb's Strategy

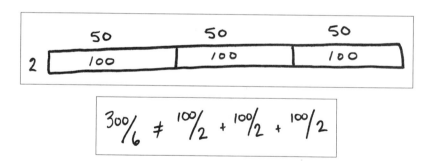

SUMMING UP . . .

When René Descartes said, "Each problem that I solved became a rule which served afterwards to solve other problems," he said it all. When children are given the chance to compute in their own ways, to play with relationships and operations, they see themselves as mathematicians and their understanding deepens. Such playing with numbers forms the basis for algebra and will take children a long way in being able to compute, not only efficiently but elegantly. Max Dehn envisioned the power of mathematical play, when he said: "Mathematics is the only instructional material that can be presented in an entirely undogmatic way." Why has it taken us so long to realize it?

8 | ASSESSMENT

If we do not change our direction, we are likely to end up where we are headed.
— Chinese Proverb

The previous chapters have documented a great deal of teaching and learning. They are filled with stories of children and teachers hard at work: children, as they construct an understanding of our number system and of multiplication and division; teachers, as they grapple with ways to facilitate this journey. The learning is evident in the conversations we have overheard and in the children's work. But is there a more formal way to assess it? And what is assessment, anyway? Is it the same thing as documentation or evaluation? And most important, what is its purpose or function?

Over the last forty years or so, answers to these questions have changed dramatically. For example, in 1967, Bloom and Foskay wrote,

> There is one field in which a considerable sophistication has developed since 1920: the field of achievement testing. It is possible now to study the degree and nature of a student's understanding of school subjects with a subtlety not previously available. Modern objective achievement tests, when properly developed and interpreted, offer one of the most powerful tools available for educational research. Findings have been made through their use that rise far above common sense. (65; cited in van den Heuvel-Panhuizen 1996)

In the fifties, sixties, and seventies, teaching and learning were seen as two separate processes. Teachers taught by transmission and feedback; learners practiced and studied. It was believed that the knowledge that resulted could be measured in terms of behavioral outcomes. Taxonomies of behavioral objectives were developed, and curricula were written to match the desired outcomes. (See the hierarchical taxonomies of Bloom et al. [1956]; and Gagné [1965].) Content was broken down into skills and subskills, which were thought to accumulate into more encompassing concepts. Teachers were expected to focus all instruction toward these outcomes, and tests were designed to measure whether learners had "mastered" them (Bloom 1980).

The language used to discuss education during this period is interesting. *Skills* refers to skillful behavior, behavior that can be executed with skill. There is certainly skill involved in hammering nails or sawing wood. One can also type skillfully. But what do we mean when we talk about mathematical "skills"? Do skills constitute mathematical thinking, or did we begin to use that terminology because skills were outcomes that were easier to measure? Certainly, if proficiency with an algorithm is the goal, one can talk of skills. But do "skills" with performing algorithms really get to the heart of mathematical *thinking*?

The term *concepts* is also grounded in behaviorism and the closely aligned psychology of associationism. One is said to have a concept of "fruit," for example, if it can be defined and associated with various exemplars—apples, peaches, etc. Back then, we assessed concepts by whether or not learners could associate exemplars—another easily measurable outcome. In mathematics, we typically used the term *concept* to refer to topics like place value or addition. We measured outcomes by determining whether learners could associate ten bundled and two loose objects with the numeral 12, for example, or whether they could arrive at correct answers to addition problems. But is this term also a misnomer when one defines mathematics as mathematizing? Clearly, concepts do not equal big ideas, nor do skills equal strategies.

And *taxonomies,* by definition, categorize knowledge into a linear framework, not a landscape. Freudenthal objected to taxonomies because he saw them as a priori categories, postulated on logical grounds by designers of curricula, tests, and measurement tools (van den Heuvel-Panhuizen 1996). He argued that they were designed to categorize problems used in achievement tests rather than to represent the genuine development of knowledge coming from a posteriori analysis of learners' work. To support his argument, he provided an example of how a taxonomy of outcomes that ascend in the order knowledge, recognition, application, integration, could actually be found in the reverse when one looks at it from the development of the learner:

> Let us follow the pattern using the knowledge of 3 < 4; this is *integrated* by, for instance, comparing one's own family of three with the family of four next door; it is *applied* to other pairs of quantities; it is *recognized* by means of a one-to-one relationship ("because they have one more child"); and it becomes *knowledge* through the counting sequence 1, 2, 3, 4. . . . (cited in van den Heuvel-Panhuizen 1996, 22)

As outcomes became the focus, *what* we assessed and *how* we assessed it were determined by what was easy to assess and measure. By emphasizing the construction of the test items, it became easy to obtain a score and use this as a measure of evaluation. Assessment moved toward evaluation, because with these so-called "objective, measurable outcomes" we now had the ability to compare learners with one another, teachers with one another, and schools with one another. The function of assessment became evaluation—both of the individual and the group. The tests provided teachers with little or no information that could inform their teaching. Although they now had a score for a learner on an achievement test, this score provided no insights into the learner's developing abilities, strategies, misconceptions, or ways of thinking. The scores were merely a quantitative way to compare learners with one another and to compare the number of correct answers with the total possible number of correct answers on a test. This ratio was assumed to be a score that reflected what students had learned.

Streefland (1981) has argued that assessment should be viewed not in the narrow sense of determining what the student has learned but from the standpoint of educational development—that it should provide teachers with information about what to teach. "Such reflective moments in education," he writes, "in which the teacher contemplates what has passed and what is still to come, are important" (35; cited in van den Heuvel-Panhuizen 1996). But the direction in the sixties and seventies was away from such common sense, toward objective measurement (Bloom and Foskay 1967). And what a path this has led us down!

Assessment outcomes today not only define what will be taught but also are used as gates to educational programs and schools. They are used to determine how much federal money schools will get. They put teachers on the line for job security and promotion. They are even used to evaluate schools and districts, thus affecting property values and the demography of neighborhoods. They are a high-stakes game. And make no mistake, they drive instruction.

Performance-Based Evaluation and Assessment

In the eighties and nineties, frameworks for teaching and learning began to shift. Emphasis was placed on learning as a constructive activity rather than as the result of transmission, practice, and reinforcement. As this new view of learning took hold, the inadequacies of the prevailing methods of assessment became apparent. In the words of Freudenthal, "We know that it is more informative to observe a student during his mathematical activity than to grade his papers" (1973, 84; cited in van den Heuvel-Panhuizen 1996).

To meet the call for more "authentic" forms of assessment, tests were made up of open-ended tasks rather than closed questions with only one answer. These performance-based assessments were designed to evaluate students' activity, *how* they went about solving a problem, rather than their answers. For example, fifth graders might be asked to solve a problem like this one:

> A playground space is being designed. It will then be blacktopped and fenced. The amount of fencing that is available for the project is 1,200 feet. Would it be better to fence a rectangular area that is longer than it is wide, or a square area? Which would give a greater area to play in? Explain and show your thinking.

Notice two important aspects of this problem. First, there are no answers to choose from. Students must solve the problem in their own way. In that sense the problem is open. Second, students are asked to explain their thinking—to show their work and justify their answer. Opening up test items in such a way shifted assessment from isolated skills and concepts to something more holistic—mathematical activity in an authentic context. Responses were quantified by applying scoring rubrics.

This performance-based assessment, while a worthy attempt to analyze student thinking, brought with it a host of problems. First, a context meaningful in one culture may not be meaningful in another. (For an urban child, playground size depends on the space available, not the amount of fencing. In many rural areas playgrounds are not fenced in at all.) Second, many of the assessment problems were written in prose and therefore depended on the learner's reading ability. Then too, second-language issues and writing facility affected learners' abilities to explain and justify their thinking. Were we assessing mathematical activity or language, culture, and writing ability? Given that the predominant use of these assessments was still evaluation of students, teachers, and schools, this was a serious issue.

PORTFOLIO-BASED DOCUMENTATION

Some researchers (Pat Carini and Ted Chittendon, among others) stepped in and suggested that assessments focus on documentation of learning rather than evaluation. Portfolio assessment was one such alternative. Samples of children's work over time were placed in portfolios and used as evidence of children's capabilities. Teachers kept anecdotal records of their observations, interviewed their students, and wrote up their reflections. All materials were placed in the portfolio as evidence of the child's mathematical thinking. These portfolios obviously documented children's mathematical activity, but how did one describe and characterize the growth? Another set of questions arose. What made a good sample entry? What kind of rubric could be used to "score" a portfolio? Was there a way to standardize the outcomes so that they could be treated as objective measures—so that they could be used for evaluation? *Should* they be used for evaluation?

ASSESSING MATHEMATIZING

The shift to performance-based assessment and the use of portfolios was a change in direction toward assessing children's mathematizing, but rather than making the mathematizing visible, we seemed to be assessing how well children could explain their strategies. What does it mean to make mathematizing visible? What is the purpose of assessment when mathematics is defined as mathematizing?

Freudenthal argued that assessment should be meaningful and provide information that will benefit the connected act of teaching:

> Examining is a meaningful activity. The teacher should be able to check the influence of the teaching process, at least in order to know how to improve it. The student has the right to know whether he has really learned something. . . . Finally there are others who are interested in knowing what somebody has learned. (1973, 83; cited in van den Heuvel-Panhuizen 1996)

From this perspective, assessment needs to inform teaching. It needs "to foresee where and how one can anticipate that which is just coming into view in the distance" (Streefland 1985, 285). It needs to capture mathematizing, not the verbal prose explaining it. It needs to assess what the child can do, not what he can't do (De Lange 1992). It needs to capture where the child is on the landscape of learning—where she has been, what her struggles are, and where she is going. It must move from being static to being dynamic (van den Heuvel-Panhuizen 1996).

Assessment must be dynamic in the sense that it evaluates *movement*—the journey. But it must also be dynamic by being *directly connected to learning and teaching*. If we teach in a way that supports mathematizing, then assessment must do the same. The information gleaned in assessment should directly inform and facilitate adjustments in teaching. For assessment to capture genuine mathematizing, for it to become dynamic, several criteria must be in place (van den Heuvel-Panhuizen 1996):

1. Students' own mathematical activity must be captured on the paper.
2. The test items must be meaningful and linked to reality.
3. Several levels of mathematizing must be possible for each item.
4. Assessment should inform teaching.

Capturing Genuine Mathematizing

There is a difference between writing about how you solved a problem and having the work visible. If teachers are to capture actual work, they need to provide scrap paper as part of the test (van den Heuvel-Panhuizen 1996). Further, requiring students to use pens rather than pencils guarantees that all marks stay visible—nothing can be erased: different starts, changes in strategies, mistakes, rewriting, final figuring, all get captured. For example,

FIGURE 8.1

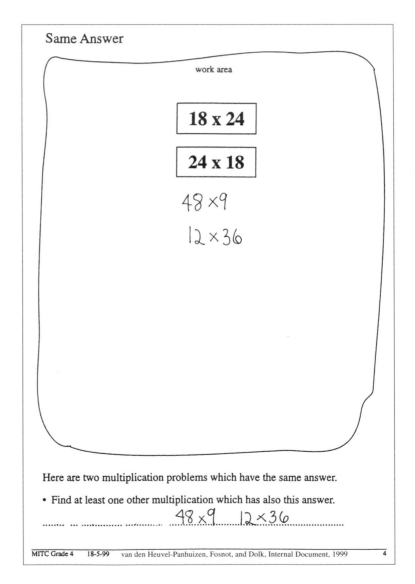

Same Answer

work area

18 x 24

24 x 18

48 ×9

12 × 36

Here are two multiplication problems which have the same answer.

• Find at least one other multiplication which has also this answer.

....   48 ×9   12 × 36 ....

MITC Grade 4   18-5-99   van den Heuvel-Panhuizen, Fosnot, and Dolk, Internal Document, 1999   4

note the three solutions in Figures 8.1, 8.2, and 8.3. The first child solves the problem mentally with doubling and halving procedures; the other two use algorithms. The second child succeeds, possibly with luck, in choosing three as a divisor. The third makes errors with the algorithm. Comparing the visible mathematizing of these three children gives the teacher a lot of useable information about where they are in the landscape of learning and the landmarks and horizons each requires.

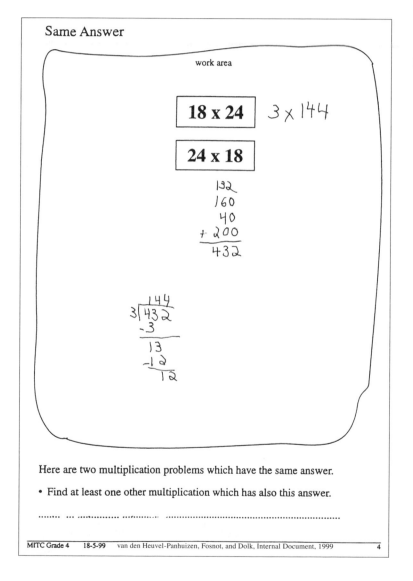

Same Answer

FIGURE 8.2

Here are two multiplication problems which have the same answer.

• Find at least one other multiplication which has also this answer.

....

Even with bare multiplication or division problems (for example, 99 × 46 or 300/12), the scrap paper captures whether children multiply 99 × 46 with an algorithm or whether they multiply by 100 and subtract 46. To solve 300 divided by 12, the scrap paper can capture whether children solve the problem mentally, perhaps by turning it into 100 divided by 4, or whether they do the long division algorithm.

FIGURE 8.3

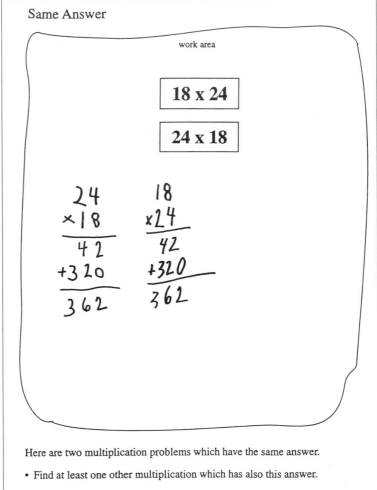

Contexts must allow children to mathematize—they must be more than word problems camouflaging "school mathematics." They must be real or be able to be imagined by children, just as the investigations used in teaching must be. One way to do this is to use pictures or tell stories (see Figure 8.4).

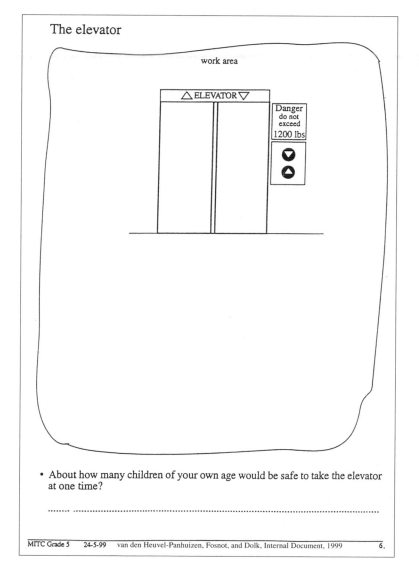

FIGURE 8.4

Providing for Various Levels of Mathematizing

The assessment items must be open enough that children can solve them in many ways. In the past, the test items themselves became progressively more difficult. One of the main problems with this approach is that "the students' behavior respects neither the taxonomies of objectives, nor the a priori analysis of difficulties" (Bodin 1993, 123; cited in van den Heuvel-Panhuizen 1996). If we want to assess levels of mathematizing, then we need, instead, to open the tasks up and look at the *way* in which the answer to the question is found, not just *whether* the answer is found. For example, there are many ways to solve the "elevator" problem in Figure 8.4. Children capable of a very high level of mathematizing would choose a reasonable estimate of the weight of a fifth grader (a friendly number related to 12, for example 60 or 80) and then reduce both the dividend and the divisor: 1,200 divided by 80 is equivalent to 300 divided by 20, which is equivalent to 30 divided by 2, which is 15. Other children might ask each classmate his or her weight, add them all up with an algorithm, then use the long division algorithm to find the average, and then use the algorithm once again to divide this average weight into 1,200. Still others might proceed randomly trying to add various weights to reach 1,200—a much lower level of mathematizing.

Informing Teaching

By assessing how a student mathematizes, teachers acquire information that enables them to determine how to proceed. They are able to understand where the child is within the landscape of learning. By analyzing the child's markings on the paper provided as part of the test, teachers are able to comprehend not only how the child is currently mathematizing but also what strategies she is trying out. The landscape of learning (which comprises strategies, big ideas, and models) informs the rubric used to analyze it but in turn also informs how it is taught. Because the landmarks become visible, teachers can determine appropriate horizons. In this way, learning and teaching are connected.

When the primary function of assessment is to inform teaching, evaluation is also redefined. Rather than "grading" schools and teachers with scores, we can characterize the mathematizing that is going on. We can evaluate the effect of various curricula and inservice professional development programs on this mathematizing. We can look at where the children are within the landscape of learning and describe the direction they need to go.

Assessing the Landscape of Learning

This book is built around a landscape of learning comprising the big ideas, strategies, and models related to multiplication and division (see Figure 8.5). As teachers assess young mathematicians in the classroom, it is the landmarks the students pass (collectively and severally) in their journey through this landscape that informs teachers' questions, their instructional decisions, and the curriculum.

The landmarks in this journey are not necessarily sequential. Many paths can be taken toward this horizon. Some landmarks are, of course, precursors to others — repeated addition is a precursor to unitizing and the distributive property. On the other hand, some children will develop computation strategies that work, like doubling and halving, before fully understanding why they work—they try out a strategy and only later construct the big idea that explains the strategy. Others will construct the big idea first. Nor is this landscape definitive, or closed. Instead it represents what we have noticed so far in the journeys in our classrooms.

As in any real journey, new landmarks can appear, and new paths, uncharted before, can be carved out. This landscape is simply a representation of others' past journeys—it can inform teaching, but it can also be added to as teachers work with the young mathematicians in their classrooms. The landmarks are not a checklist or a list of behavioral outcomes. They are a means to focus on and describe students' mathematizing.

Assessing in the Moment

The best and perhaps most valid assessment happens while teaching and learning are taking place. As students interact in the classroom (with their teacher and with other students), as situations are explored and mathematized, teachers can observe the landmarks being passed. If teachers understand the landscape well, they become better able to observe, confer, and question in relation to important mathematical ideas, strategies, and models—to maximize mathematical teaching moments.

Anecdotal records document the journey, but they are also helpful reminders that can inform teaching. For example, let's look at this note jotted down by Maxine, a fourth-grade teacher:

> I noticed that Peter made a big leap today. We were building boxes that would hold 36 chocolates. At first he began in a trial-and-error fashion, building all the boxes that he could think of that worked. But when he began to record, he systematically turned each box, labeling the different ways the box could be held. I suggested that he put parentheses around the array that he

FIGURE 8.5 *Landscape of Learning: Multiplication and Division on the Horizon Showing Landmark Strategies (Rectangles), Big Ideas (Ovals), and Models (Triangles)*

was using for the base of the box. He then began to notate each possibility systematically and to proceed with all the possibilities with one layer, then all the possibilities with two layers, and so on. [See Figure 8.6.] When he had finished recording I congratulated him on his system and asked him if he thought it would be possible to know now ahead of time all the possibilities for 36 candies, without having to build all the boxes. Could he use his parentheses system? Together we wrote the first arrangement: $1 \times 2 \times 18$. He broke the 18 into 2×9. I suggested that he continue and break the 9 down further into 3×3. Now he had $1 \times 2 \times 2 \times 3 \times 3$. He began to use the parentheses, moving it around to all the possibilities, missing some, but attempting to be systematic!

Maxine's anecdotal records document her instructional choice that day when she suggested using parentheses and urged Peter to continue factoring to the prime factors. And her notes will serve as a reminder to her that tomorrow she wants to encourage Peter to continue to factor amounts down to the primes—a very important idea underlying number theory.

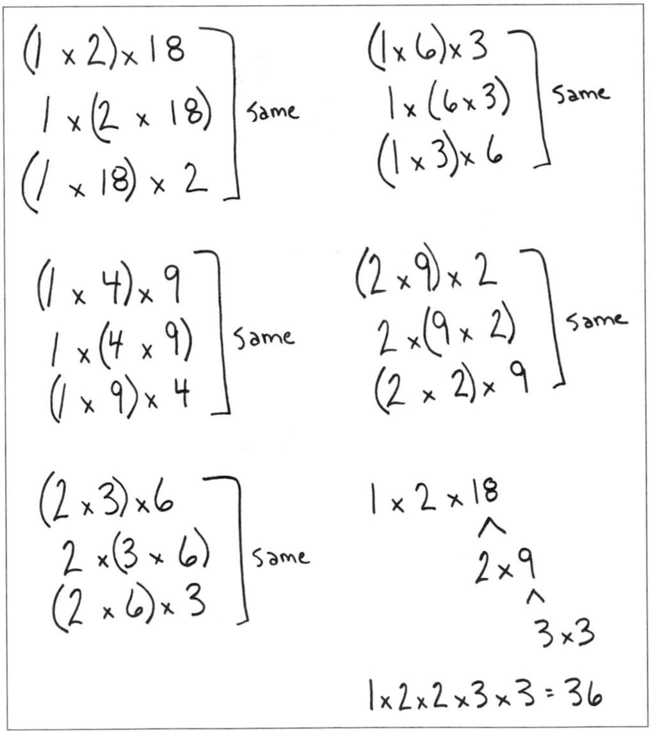

FIGURE 8.6
Peter's Work

Teachers can involve children in choosing and putting samples of work into a portfolio. Throughout the year, work can be dated and comments can be made in relation to the landscape. For example, Maxine might discuss Peter's work on the box problem with him. Together they might note how he had known the various arrangements and reflect together on the system he is developing based on the associative property and prime factoring—an important landmark. Over the course of the year, Peter's portfolio will become full of entries that serve as evidence of his mathematizing—and his development as a young mathematician.

Paper and Pencil Assessments

As long as the test items are designed in relation to the criteria described in this chapter, paper-and-pencil tests can provide important information for both students and teachers. For example, noting how children solve $600 \div 48$ or 25×12 on their scrap paper helps teachers see whether children are making use of number relations as they calculate. Six hundred divided by forty-eight can be solved by tinkering with number relations: $\frac{1}{2}$ of $100 \div 4$, or $600 \div 50 + \frac{1}{2}$, or $100 \div 8$. Twenty-five times twelve can be solved as $\frac{1}{4}$ of 12×100, or 50×6, or 100×3; on the other hand, some children may still need to take smaller leaps, such as $(10 \times 12) + (10 \times 12) + (5 \times 12)$, or even use repeated addition of twenty-five twelve times. Still others may not use relationships at all but rewrite the problem vertically in order to perform an algorithm. The scrap paper provides evidence of the strategy.

ASSESSMENT RESULTS

Mathematizing

How do children in classrooms like those depicted in this book compare with children in traditional classrooms, in which mathematics is taught as procedures? To look at this question, an assessment with items that were open enough to capture various levels of mathematizing (van den Heuvel-Panhuizen, Fosnot, and Dolk 1999) was given to third, fourth, and fifth graders in classrooms in which the Mathematics in the City program was being well implemented. The same assessment was given to third, fourth, and fifth graders in the same schools or district, who had been taught algorithms and given little opportunity to mathematize. Responses were coded with a rubric that reflected the landscape of learning.

The children's answers were not significantly different; however, their position within the landscape of learning differed remarkably (van den Heuvel-Panhuizen 2000). Children in classrooms in which number relationships and context were emphasized outperformed their traditionally taught peers significantly in using strategies representative of number sense. They easily composed and decomposed numbers to make them friendly, frequently computing mentally. Traditionally taught children relied on algorithms no matter what the numbers were. Children in reformed classrooms treated answers to problems within the context. For example, when asked to figure out how many children could fit in the elevator, most of these children responded by choosing a body weight that was related to 1,200 (see Figure 8.7a). Many of the traditionally taught children responded by using the algorithm to make a calculation, performing an incorrect op-

FIGURE 8.7a

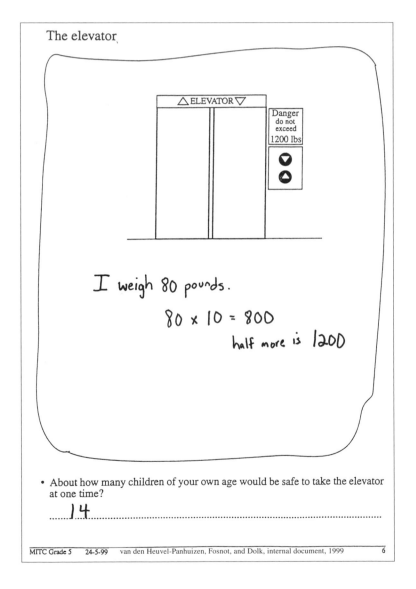

The elevator

I weigh 80 pounds.

80 × 10 = 800

half more is 1200

• About how many children of your own age would be safe to take the elevator at one time?

14

MITC Grade 5   24-5-99   van den Heuvel-Panhuizen, Fosnot, and Dolk, internal document, 1999   6

eration, or in some cases coming up with answers with remainders (which in context make no sense—see Figure 8.7b).

Standardized Tests Results

Unfortunately most school districts are still held accountable on state and city standardized tests. In New York City, this test is the Terra Nova. It is a multiple-choice standardized achievement test similar to those used by most school districts. We again compared third, fourth, and fifth graders

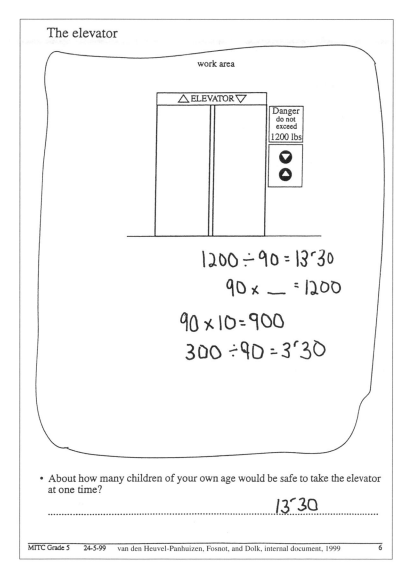

FIGURE 8.7b

based on the results of this test and found a difference significant at the .0001 level (Fosnot et al. 2001). The fourth-grade test results were of particular interest: the mean score of Mathematics in the City children fell in the middle of level three, the level considered proficient by New York State. The mean of the traditionally taught students fell within level two, a level below proficiency. Also, item analysis of the fifth-grade tests showed Mathematics in the City students to rate significantly higher on number understanding, geometry, measurement, data, and problem solving. (The difference on computation was not significant, although the mean score of Mathematics in the City children was higher.)

We share these results not because we believe standardized tests are the best way to assess learning. We don't, and we have tried to make that clear in this chapter. It is often argued, however, that change cannot occur in light of the pressure brought to bear because standardized assessments are used. Many districts mandate that teachers teach to the test. Pacing calendars aligned with the standardized tests determine curriculum in these districts, and direct instruction, practice, and test preparation characterize these classrooms. When this happens, assessment drives instruction and children are taught only the kind of thinking that can easily be assessed by these tests. They are not taught to think, to mathematize. Our data are proof that the practice of teaching to the test is a misappropriation of time. If children are taught in a way that allows them to construct understanding, they will perform better, even on standardized tests.

SUMMING UP . . .

The Chinese proverb used as the epigraph to this chapter states, "If we do not change our direction, we are likely to end up where we are headed." If we teach directly to standardized achievement tests, we may end up with children who can pass them but who know little mathematics. If we want to encourage mathematizing and the development of number relationships, we need to teach in a way that supports it.

Early attempts at assessment were driven by learning based on behaviorism and the belief that tests could measure this learning objectively. As our concept of learning shifted to include a deeper understanding of cognitive development, one characterized by constructivism, these tests were seen as insufficient. Performance-based assessment and portfolios replaced earlier tests. Problems arose, however, over whether we were assessing language or mathematics and how to quantify scores on portfolios.

Assessments need to inform teaching, and they need to reflect mathematizing. If assessments are developed that make mathematizing visible and include realistic items that can be mathematized on many levels, they can be beneficial. They can document the journey toward the horizon of numeracy. The landscape of learning can serve as a framework, since it depicts important landmarks. However, it should not be seen as a list of outcomes but as a representation of many children's past journeys.

When young mathematicians are hard at work, they are thinking, they become puzzled, they become intrigued: they are learning to see their world through a mathematical lens. Assessment needs to capture the learning this lens reveals.

9 | TEACHERS AS MATHEMATICIANS

*Life is good for only two things, discovering
mathematics and teaching mathematics.*

—Siméon Poisson

*Gel'fand amazed me by talking of mathematics as
though it were poetry. He once said about a long
paper bristling with formulas that it contained the
vague beginnings of an idea which he could only hint
at, and which he had never managed to bring out
more clearly. I had always thought of mathematics
as being much more straightforward: a formula is a
formula, and an algebra is an algebra, but Gel'fand
found hedgehogs lurking in the rows of his spectral
sequences!*

—Dusa McDuff

TEACHER PREPARATION

So far this book has focused on *young* mathematicians at work—children
between the ages of seven and ten hard at work constructing, questioning,
mathematizing, and communicating their world through a mathematical
lens. But if teachers are to be able to facilitate mathematical journeys for the
young learners with whom they work, they too need to have a strong understanding of the subject. To this end, teacher education programs in the
United States have added more and more mathematics courses. Over the
last ten years there has been an impetus to make a liberal arts undergradu-
ate degree a requirement for certification. Usually this has meant that education programs have been reduced to a single year (thirty credits) so that a
bachelor of arts degree can still be obtained in four years or a master of arts
in five. In essence, the trend has been to increase the length of the overall
program, increase the number of liberal arts courses, and decrease the number of education courses. Today, teachers in the United States are required
to take more college mathematics courses than ever before, yet the gap between the needed and the actual content understanding seems to be widen-
ing. The cry for inservice professional development has now become a roar.
Why are our teachers so ill prepared?

Some critics blame the teachers. They push for stricter entrance re-
quirements for teacher education programs—higher grade-point averages

and better scores on entrance examinations. Many states have developed their own examinations and introduced tiered certifications—initial, provisional, permanent, professional. A master's degree is often necessary in order to receive a permanent license, and salaries have been raised. All of these reforms have produced little real change in teachers' competence in mathematics.

Teacher educators in the Netherlands have taken a different tack. People who want to become primary school teachers in the Netherlands do not attend a university, pursue a liberal arts degree, or take courses in a mathematics department. Instead, they attend *Hogeschool,* a four-year post–high school program specifically focused on teacher preparation. During the four years, students take seven or eight courses in mathematics education, courses geared toward a deep understanding of the mathematical topics *they will be teaching.* Prospective teachers learn about the big ideas embedded in the topics, about how children's strategies develop, about important mathematical models. They learn about the role of context and how to use didactical models like the open array. They explore number patterns and mental math strategies. They become strong mathematical thinkers *in relation to the topics they will be teaching*—the landscape they will travel through with their children. But is even this enough?

Korthagen and Kessel (1999) have argued that a major problem with teacher education programs is that they are grounded in theory and methods, in *episteme,* and what is taught does not transfer to the classroom. Prospective teachers have preconceptions about learning and teaching that come from their past experiences as students. These preconceptions are so strong they prove resistant to new learning, particularly when the new learning is divorced from practice. It's true that most teacher decision making is split second and grounded in perception, feelings, interpretation, and reaction (Dolk 1997). Teachers respond based on their subconscious beliefs about teaching and learning and on their overall vision of practice—beliefs and a vision developed during many years of being learners themselves, most often in classrooms in which mathematics was defined as a discipline to be transmitted.

Teachers who are already in the classroom are rarely different. Although they have more experience, their belief systems are often not aligned with the belief systems implicit in the new curricula or in education reform. John is typical. Asked about his beliefs about teaching he says, "How do I view the process of teaching? Part actor, part salesman. You have this body of knowledge that you have to get across to kids, but most students really don't want to be in school, so you have to sell them on this education kick. If you don't make your presentation good and you're not a good actor, they're not going to buy" (Fosnot 1993). Unless these beliefs are challenged and modified, when John is given new curricula based on constructivism, he will assume that the purpose of problem solving is to motivate children. He will see activity as important to promote interest. He will adapt new pedagogical strategies, but he will see them as new strategies to help him "get the body of knowledge across."

How do we help teachers (both preservice and inservice) develop a new conception of the nature of mathematics, one based on the human activity of making meaning through a mathematical lens? How do we revise the picture of what should be happening in the classroom? These two questions get at the heart of what is required in teacher education if reform is to be successful. Providing teachers with new textbooks or new pedagogical strategies will produce only superficial changes. The new strategies will be implemented within the constructs of the belief systems teachers already hold.

To get John and teachers like him to analyze and reflect on their beliefs, teacher education itself must undergo radical change. It needs to be grounded in new visions of practice based on how students learn. This often means creating disequilibrium with regard to prior conceptions. Rather than basing our work with teachers on *episteme*, we need to look to a framework based on *phronesis* and *constructivism* (Fosnot 1989, 1993, 1996; Korthagen and Kessel 1999). *Phronesis* is situation-specific knowledge related to the context in which it is used—in this case, the process of teaching and learning. Constructivism describes learning as the process of building one's own understanding by modifying prior schemes and structures. Rather than teaching teachers about theory, which we then expect them to apply, we need to give them experiences that involve action, reflection, and conversation within the context of teaching and learning. They need to construct new beliefs, a new vision of what it means to teach and learn mathematics. They need to experience an environment in which mathematics is taught as mathematizing and learning is seen as constructing.

When teachers themselves model situations mathematically, construct solutions, set up relationships, and defend their ideas to their peers, their vision of mathematics pedagogy and their definition of mathematics begin to shift. By reflecting on their own learning and what facilitated it, they begin to form new beliefs—ones that often contradict prior beliefs. These beliefs in turn will become the basis for the way in which they react, question, and interact during learning/teaching moments. Teachers also need more situation-specific knowledge that can inform their decision making—more knowledge about how children develop mathematical ideas and strategies, a better ability to see and understand the mathematics in children's work. They need to understand mathematics as the human activity of mathematizing. And they need to understand the landscape of learning.

Throughout this book we have shown you teachers who define mathematics as mathematizing, who value their students' mathematical ideas and strategies, who promote genuine mathematical discourse within a community of mathematicians. These teachers walk the edge between the structure of mathematics and student development, between the individual and the community. In fact, they are willing to *live* on the edge, not always knowing the direction the path will take—to challenge themselves mathematically.

They have acquired an in-depth understanding of the mathematical topics they teach and of the landscape of learning—the big ideas, the strategies, and the models. But they have done more. They have come to see themselves as mathematicians, to understand that mathematics is the human activity of mathematizing. They have learned to mathematize their world.

LEARNING TO MATHEMATIZE

Once again, the most vivid way for us to show you what we mean is to have you listen in during a teacher education session as the participants grapple with some mathematical ideas and then reflect on their learning and teaching.

Exploring the Edge

It's the first day of a Mathematics in the City summer institute. Cathy Fosnot, one of the instructors, has asked the participants (all elementary teachers), in groups of six or seven, to introduce themselves to one another. Each person is to identify one thing he or she has in common with each other member of the group. Each group is then to figure out the number of these "connections" for their group and predict the number of connections for the entire class, for the entire institute, for *any-sized group.*

Although on the surface this may appear a simple multiplicative situation similar to others described in this book, it is much more difficult. Opening the context to include any-sized group prompts the participants to investigate it much more deeply, to explore the many different ways the situation can be modeled, and to construct algebraic expressions and representations. They are being asked to be learners in a mathematical environment.

"There's a pattern . . . you just subtract one each time," Barbara, a third-grade teacher, explains to the other five members of her group. "See, I made a connection with each of you, so that was five. Then Roger made four, because he doesn't count himself, and he's already made a connection with me. Mary, you made three. Kasia made two. Sherrie, you only had to make one, because you've already made connections with everyone I've already mentioned. And, Kelly, you didn't make any, because we've all made connections with you already!" Kelly feigns a frown, and everyone laughs.

"Then we add them all up, and that is how many connections we've made," Roger agrees and excitedly adds, "so if our group had one hundred members, it would be ninety-nine plus ninety-eight plus ninety-seven . . . all the way to one!" On a large piece of paper, Roger writes, "For a group of 100: Start with 99 and keep subtracting one. Then add it all up."

Kasia asks, "But what about for any-sized group? There's got to be a more general way to write it."

"Right. There's a pattern," Mary says. "It doesn't matter what the size of the group is . . . it's always a descending order, and it will keep going like that. Couldn't we write $n - 1 + n - 2 + n - 3$, and so on?"

"Oh, great idea." Roger enthusiastically adds Mary's suggestion to the chart that he has started: "For any-sized group, call it n, the number of connections will be $(n - 1) + (n - 2) + (n - 3) + (n - 4). . . .$" But now Roger looks puzzled. "How do I write when you stop?" he asks in exasperation. The group ponders his dilemma.

"Maybe it's to infinity," Sherrie offers. "The numbers we are subtracting keep getting bigger."

Although Sherrie is intrigued with the patterns the group is noticing and is using them to generate additional numbers, she is not considering *why* the patterns are happening. This keeps her from generalizing in relation to n. This often happens when learners are investigating. Patterns intrigue them, and they use them. Often they assume a pattern will continue even though they have seen it in a limited number of examples. To really understand the pattern, to prove the relationships in order to generalize beyond the limited number of examples (in other words, to mathematize), the relationships in the pattern must be defined and quantified. However, noticing patterns is often the beginning of a good mathematical question—one that leads mathematicians to consider why patterns are happening and whether they will always happen in that specifically defined situation.

In algebra, one symbol—x, for example—can mean many things. That's why we call it a variable. But when we set up an equation using these symbols, the *relationships* represented are specific. The *definition* of the variable is also specific. Here's Lichtenberg on the power of algebraic language: "In mathematical analysis we call x the undetermined part of line a: the rest we don't call y, as we do in common life, but $a - x$. Hence mathematical language has great advantages over the common language" (Woodard 2000). The symbols used in algebra are defined *in relationship to* one another. And this gets right to the heart of mathematics—the describing and quantifying of relationships. These teachers are struggling to do this—to describe in algebraic language the mathematical relationships they are noticing.

Kasia relates the increasing and decreasing patterns back to the context, back to the situation. "No, that can't be. That might be more than the number of people in the group! What gets subtracted has to relate back to the number of people in the group."

"Wouldn't it be $n - (n - 1)$?" Roger writes the expression as he talks. "That would be subtracting one less than the number in the group, so that would give us one. And that's where we stop."

"But that's a negative number," Sherrie puzzles, "n minus n equals zero. Take away one and you get negative one."

So often we take for granted that because teachers have had algebra courses and can manipulate algebraic equations, their understanding is solid. But so much of the mathematics teachers have learned in their past schooling is procedural; almost never have they been asked to *construct* mathematics. Further, the procedures they learned were taught by explanation. Often even the basic prealgebraic ideas are not really understood.

"No, it's not," Roger explains. "It's within parentheses, so a minus times a minus is a plus. So it's *n* minus *n,* which is zero, plus one. Although I've never understood why," he adds, laughing sheepishly.

Kelly joins in. "I have no idea why either," she laughs. "But what I do know is that I made *no* connections because when we got to me I had already made a connection with everyone, remember? Why don't we just write $(n - 1) + (n - 2) + (n - 3) \ldots (n - n)$? That would take us to zero."

"Yeah, that's good!" Roger agrees and writes down Kelly's suggestion.

Everyone at the table seems satisfied until Barbara comments, "This works, but you know it's still a lot of work to add all these numbers up . . . like ninety-nine plus ninety-eight plus ninety-seven, all the way to zero. There must be a faster way. . . ." Puzzled once again, the group ponders Barbara's point.

The drive for elegance, simplicity, and efficiency is important in mathematics. It is just this drive that causes mathematicians to describe their inventions as creative, as beautiful. As they pare a problem down to its "bones" and represent the relationships with mathematical language, they create a mathematical representation that can be used to model the situation. This activity gets to the heart of what it means to mathematize reality. The situation can now be seen through the lens of this mathematical structure. These teachers are grappling with a way to simplify their work.

At a nearby table another group is having a similar discussion. They explain their ideas to Cathy, who has joined them.

"We tried lots of different-sized groups, and we know that each time a new person enters the group, the number of connections increases by the number of people already in the group," Stephanie says.

Cathy paraphrases to clarify. "So, for example, if a group of five people can make ten connections, to determine the number of connections for a group of six people, you just add five and ten? Do you know why?"

"Sure," Jadine responds. "Because that person will need to make a connection with each group member, one less than the number of people in the new group. She can't make a connection with herself. Our problem is that this is very cumbersome. You have to know the total number of connections for the group that is one less in order to make use of this strategy. Like you have to know the number of connections for ninety-nine people in order to figure the total for a group of one hundred! It's not very efficient."

Cathy agrees, laughing along with them and encouraging them to continue looking for a more efficient strategy. "Collecting data for various-sized groups was a great way to start, and by doing so you noticed patterns in the data that enabled you to come up with the strategy you have. Why don't you try organizing your work so far with a table and continue looking for relationships? Maybe you could explore the relationship between the number of people and the number of connections in a third column." She draws the table shown in Figure 9.1.

Cathy is being rather leading here, hoping the group will explore the ratio between people and connections and grapple with the multiplicative structure. Should she have let the group construct a way to organize their work themselves? Clearly there is benefit in that, too; deciding how to organize one's work is an important aspect of mathematics. By suggesting an organizing strategy, Cathy does not allow the participants to construct one for themselves. On the other hand, they do begin to construct further relationships. Teaching in a way that supports a journey across a landscape requires a lot of decisions, and there are pros and cons at each critical point. As we guide learners, our decisions often determine the paths they will take. Is Cathy being too leading? It depends. The critical issue is whether the group takes ownership of the work and continues constructing mathematics.

Jadine immediately becomes excited. "Look! I see a relationship between the odd ones. For a group of three, it's three connections. For a group of five, it's ten connections. That's double. Then for seven, it's twenty-one. That's triple! See. The next one is four times it! It's a growing pattern!"

Stephanie is impressed with Jadine's discovery and elaborates on it. "If we could determine the relationship number ahead of time, we could

# People	Relationship	# Connections
3	1	3
4	1.5	6
5	2	10
6	2.5	15

FIGURE 9.1
Constructing a Ratio Table

multiply it by the number of people and we would know the number of connections!"

"What happens with the even?" Cathy asks.

At first everyone is perplexed, but Clarissa finally ventures an explanation. "If we divide the connections by the number of people in the group we get the relationship number. So for four people, it's six divided by four. That's one point five. For six people, it's fifteen divided by six. That's two point five."

"Oh, my gosh, I got it! I got it!" Jadine is triumphant. "If you take one away from the total number in the group and divide that amount by two, you get the relationship number! It doesn't matter if the group is even or odd! The relationship number is *n* minus one divided by two, if *n* is the number of people in the group!"

"Jadine, that's great! So all we have to do is multiply *n* minus one divided by two by the number of people in the group, *n*, and we get the number of connections!" Stephanie quickly writes a formula: $n(n-1)/2$.

Cathy moves to Barbara's group, still hard at work looking for a simpler strategy. On their paper, they have written several examples of descending series (see Figure 9.2). They are now discussing simpler ways to add them.

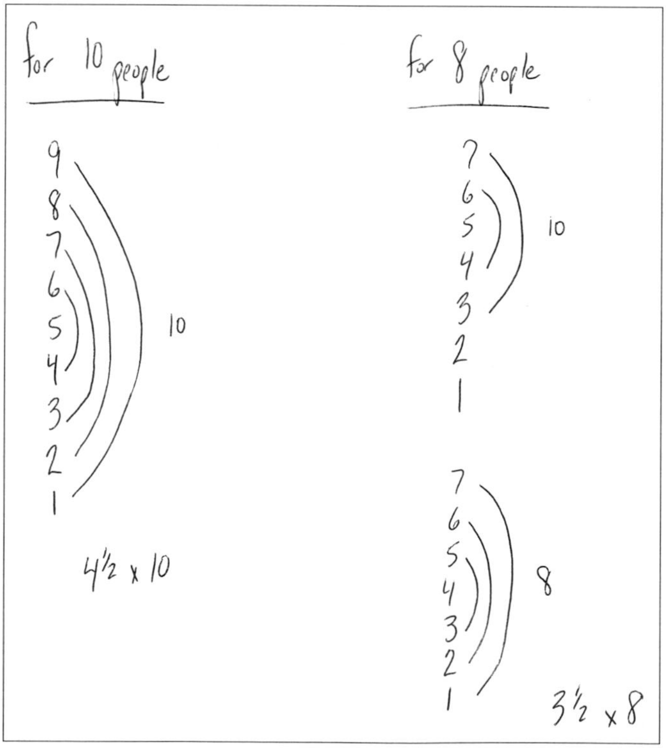

FIGURE 9.2
Barbara, Kelly, and Roger's Pairing Strategy

"Making tens is easier," Kelly notes. "See. You can pair the nine and one, and the eight and two, and so forth. That makes four and a half groups of ten. The five doesn't get a partner, but it's half of ten."

Roger begins to make tens with the descending series for eight people. "Seven and three, six and four, but where does this get us? The others—five, two, and one—don't add up to ten. They make eight. How does this help?"

Barbara laughs and jokingly replies, "Why don't you make eights?"

Roger starts to laugh but then sees that her idea will work. "Hey, it works. Seven and one, six and two, five and three, and four is left. Half of eight! Three and a half groups of eight!"

They begin to record their results, labeling one of their columns "# pairs" (see Figure 9.3). Cathy moves on to see how another group is modeling the problem. Sam, Joan, Maria, Joaquin, Rachel, and Eliza have used Unifix cubes of different colors to represent the connections they each made, and they have drawn a representation of the groups on paper.

# People	# Connections	# Pairs
10	45	4.5
8	28	3.5

FIGURE 9.3

"Each group member stands for a point," Eliza explains to Cathy. "See? And the colored lines are the connections." She points to their drawings, shown in Figure 9.4. "Because there were six of us, we made a hexagon." They have drawn various polygons and shown all the connections as line segments—a powerful geometric modeling of the situation.

Maria continues. "I was yellow, and I had five connections. Sam was green, and he made four. Joan was red; she made three. Joaquin was orange; he made two. Rachel was brown; she made one."

"And I had none," Eliza concludes with a laugh.

"This is great, what you are doing," Cathy comments. "Have you thought about a way to generalize this? Is there any relationship between the number of points and the number of line segments—the connections you can make?"

Cathy leaves them to ponder that question and notices that the group at the adjacent table has also employed a geometric model: using graph paper, they have drawn a square with each of their names across the top and then down the side (see Figure 9.5).

"What a terrific way to model the situation," Cathy comments when she sees what they have done.

"What's really neat is what we are working on now." Bob, a fourth-grade teacher, speaks for the group. "We did this first just to organize our think-

FIGURE 9.4

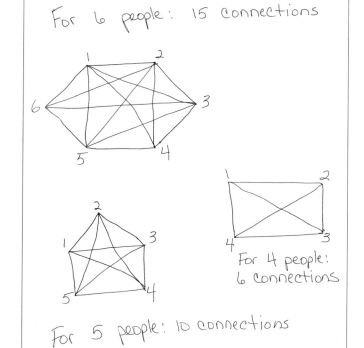

ing. But what we have noticed by doing this is that it always makes a square, and the diagonal is always the number of people in the group, because they do not make a connection with themselves."

"Right." Jasmine picks up where Bob left off. "And the connections that count are half of what's left when you subtract out the diagonal! So we worked on a formula to express this: *n* squared minus *n*, all divided by two," she finishes with a flourish. "I haven't thought this hard about math in a long, long time."

Formulating a Vision

Algebra came about because mathematicians needed to communicate their ideas to one another—to communicate the relationships they noticed. Algebraic symbols can be used in many ways, and mathematicians decide for themselves what relationships to express and how to express them. For teachers to appreciate the feeling of empowerment that comes from building an idea for oneself and to be able to generate this same feeling in their students, they must experience the process. They must learn what it means to work at the edge of their knowledge, to challenge themselves mathematically, to think hard. They must learn that puzzlement is an important process in learning. Teachers must be willing to see themselves as mathematicians and to understand that mathematics is a creative process—one that

FIGURE 9.5

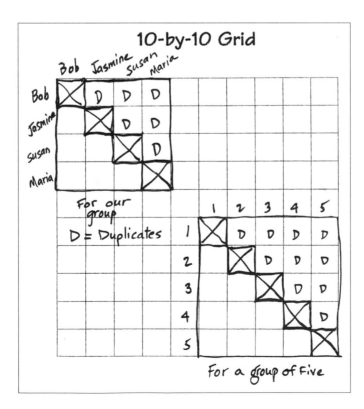

often demands a struggle. Only then will they really understand the exhilaration and empowerment that comes from doing mathematics—from constructing and mathematizing their world.

Because teachers usually believe that teaching means explaining clearly or that learners will learn if they listen and try to understand what is being explained, they often think a "math congress" is nothing more than a whole-class "share"—a time when learners try to explain their thinking to one another. Although this is partially true—learners do try to explain their thinking—the purpose of the discussion is to continue to deepen everyone's mathematical understanding, particularly those who are sharing, not for some to tell so others will "get it." If learning involves constructing and making sense of ideas for oneself, then telling has little effect, even when one learner is telling another. The teacher must think through the purpose of the congress and orchestrate the sharing accordingly.

Even though these teachers have experienced the joy of constructing ideas for themselves in group work, they still need to experience the process of discussing critical mathematical ideas, exploring similarities between solutions, and modeling situations in alternative ways.

With this in mind, Cathy convenes a math congress and asks Jadine's group to present their solution first. They post their chart showing the middle column of "relationship numbers" and explaining how they arrived at the formula $n(n-1)/2$.

"But I don't understand what the n minus one over two means in the situation," says Jasmine. "Is it connections or people? I'm confused." Jasmine's group has constructed the formula $(n^2 - n)/2$, and she understands it in the context of the graph-paper array. Although Jadine's group has done some beautiful work, they have not grappled yet with *why* the pattern occurs. Jasmine's question pushes them to explain the pattern, not just to represent it algebraically.

Stephanie tries to respond. "We didn't do it that way. We made a relationship between the people and the connections. This number is the relationship."

"I know," Jasmine retorts, "but still I want to know why that relationship happens."

"I think our group can explain," says Barbara. "We have the same formula. Can we share what we did?" Barbara, Roger, Kelly, Sherrie, Kasia, and Mary come forward, and each demonstrates the pairing of a different series. When they have finished, they explain how the pairing produces the same number of pairs as the first group's "relationship number."

Jasmine is still not satisfied. "That helps me understand a little more why the relationship is happening, but it still seems abstract. Our solution makes so much more sense to me."

"What did your group do?" Barbara asks.

"We made a square. We made every possibility, then we subtracted out ourselves, the diagonal, and divided by two to get rid of the duplicates."

This group's modeling of the situation is easily understood because it is so connected to the context: the representation is clear. Cathy wants to en-

courage everyone to think about the connections across solutions, however, so she asks the whole group to explain how the various solutions are
connected.

"I can see algebraically how they are connected," Roger begins. "If
you multiply our algebraic expression out, you get theirs: $n \times (n - 1) = (n^2 - n)$."

"Can you show the relationship on their model, Roger?"

Many faces take on puzzled looks.

Finally Sam asks tentatively, "Can I use scissors and cut your model?"
Sam comes forward and cuts out the diagonal, collapsing the square into a
rectangular array of the dimensions $n \times (n - 1)$.

"Oh, wow." "Great!" "Of course!" Many voices acknowledge understanding.

Sam continues, "What I just realized as I saw this, was the answer to my
own struggle." He explains. "We made polygons in my group of all the connections, but I had trouble generalizing to a formula. What I just now realized is that all the possibilities, if you don't worry about duplicates, can be
represented by multiplication. It's just $n \times (n - 1)$. It's simple multiplication, because everyone can have a connection with everyone except themselves. So if the group has six members there are six times five possible connections. Then you just divide by two to get rid of the duplicates."

Jasmine is satisfied. "What is so nice, Sam, is how you built on our solution. You gave me new insights, too. There are so many ways to model this
situation. I am so amazed at what we all did."

Several teachers comment that they had studied combinations previously in school and knew they could be expressed by a descending algebraic
series, but that it had little meaning to them. They also had been taught procedures to multiply $n \times (n - 1)$ with little understanding of how that might
look in an array. Their mathematical understanding is being deepened, and
they are also beginning to think deeply about their beliefs about teaching
and learning. They are beginning to formulate new visions of practice.

Living in a Mathematical World

Being a mathematician means thinking about mathematics outside the classroom as well as in it. It means being willing to work on problems at home,
to wonder about them during your commute to work, to raise your own
mathematical inquiries. Toward this end, we ask teachers in our workshops
and courses to keep double-entry journals. On one side they are to continue
the mathematics they have been doing during the day—reflect on other
participants' mathematical ideas, do more work on ideas they did not fully
understand, raise other questions and/or mathematical inquiries. (We often
form inquiry groups around these mathematical questions and pursue them
during the institutes.) The other side of the journal is for recording insights about learning and teaching—what enabled them to learn the things
they learned, what strategies they might try in their classrooms to help children learn. These pedagogical insights should be connected to the insights

related to their own learning: that's why it's a *double*-entry journal. Our aim is to enable teachers to form new beliefs, a new vision of practice, and then help them transform these beliefs into practical strategies—to ground teacher education in an analysis of the connection between learning and teaching.

After the class we've discussed in this chapter, Sam wrote in the mathematics side of his journal:

> I didn't really understand what *n* was in the equations at first. It wasn't until I saw the array that Jasmine presented that it clicked. And then all last night I was thinking about our polygons. About how any number of points in space could be represented by connecting line segments, the total being $n(n-1)$ over 2. It made me think about cities and possible connecting roads. It's the same. Then I couldn't sleep, and I turned on the *Late Show,* and there was Letterman with all his guests, and I thought, "Oh, my god, the number of handshakes if they all shake hands is $n(n-1)$ divided by 2." And I see it as a rectangle. Does that mean that the number is always a triangle, if it's half a rectangle?

The use of array models is a powerful picture for Sam. Liebniz once commented, "In symbols one observes an advantage in discovery which is greatest when they express the exact nature of a thing briefly and, as it were, picture it; then indeed the labor of thought is wonderfully diminished." Sam continues using the array and draws several of the examples:

> Of course. I can arrange all of these answers into a triangle. [*He draws three dots and shows how it grows each time when the next row is added.*] Three becomes six. Six becomes ten. Ten becomes fifteen. Wow.

Then, on the pedagogical side of his double-entry journal, Sam reflects on how his own learning will affect his teaching:

> Math was never like this for me. I remember sitting in school with my head bent and my hands cupped around my work so no one could see it. My job was to try and understand the teacher's explanation and then solve the problems on the sheet. What a joy it was today to work as a community. I hope I can give my kids the same kind of experience. I feel exhilarated and empowered to figure out things for myself. I feel like a mathematician and I want my kids to have that same feeling.

Sam is beginning to see himself as a mathematician. He is willing to raise and pursue mathematical inquiries—to see the world through a mathematical lens. He is enjoying and appreciating the puzzlement that accompanies genuine learning.

The mathematician Alfred Renyi once commented, "If I feel unhappy, I do mathematics to become happy. If I am happy, I do mathematics to keep happy" (Woodard 2000). Perhaps it is too much to expect to turn every teacher into someone who derives as much joy in doing mathematics as Renyi did. But math anxiety can be lessened when teachers are able to appreciate and take pleasure in creating and figuring out mathematics.

SUMMING UP . . .

For teachers to be able to teach in the ways illustrated in these chapters, they need to walk the edge between the structure of mathematics and child development, between the community and the individual. They need to be willing to live on the edge, mathematically speaking. There is no one path, no one line, no one map for the journey. The landscape of learning has many paths, and the horizons shift as we approach them. Knowing the landscape, having a sense of the landmarks—the big ideas, the strategies, and the models—helps us plan the journey. We need to structure the environment to bring children closer to the landmarks, to the horizon—to enable them to act on their world mathematically.

Just as mathematics learning needs to be situated in context, in the environment of the landscape, teacher education needs to be situated in the context of teaching/learning. New belief systems and a new vision of practice need to be constructed through subsequent reflection on learning and teaching. Teachers need to see themselves as mathematicians. If we foster environments in which teachers can begin to see mathematics as mathematizing—as constructing mathematical meaning in their lived world—they will be better able to facilitate the journey for the young mathematicians with whom they work.

REFERENCES

BAKER, H. F. Quoted in Cajori, F. 1999. *A History of Mathematics*. New York: Chelsea.

BATTISTA, M. T., D. H. CLEMENTS, J. ARNOFF, K. BATTISTA, AND C. VAN DEN BORROW. 1998. "Students' Spatial Structuring of Two-Dimensional Arrays of Squares." *Journal for Research in Mathematics Education* 29(5): 503–32.

BEISHUIZEN, M., K. P. E. GRAVEMEIJER, AND E. C. D. M. VAN LIESHOUT. 1997. *The Role of Contexts and Models in the Development of Mathematical Strategies and Procedures*. Series on Research in Education, no. 26 (CD-ß Press). Utrecht, the Netherlands: Utrecht University.

BELL, E. T. 1987. *Mathematics, Queen and Servant of Science*. New York: Mathematics Association of America.

BLOOM, B. S. 1980. *All Our Children Learning*. New York: McGraw-Hill.

BLOOM, B. S., AND A. W. FOSKAY. 1967. "Formulation of Hypotheses." In *International Study of Achievement in Mathematics. A Comparison in Twelve Countries,* edited by T. Huson, vol. 1, 64–76. Stockholm: Almqvist and Wiskell.

BLOOM, B. S., J. T. HASTINGS, AND G. F. MADAUS. 1971. *Handbook on Formative and Summative Evaluation of Student Learning*. New York: McGraw-Hill.

BODIN, A. 1993. "What Does 'to Assess' Mean? The Case of Assessing Mathematical Knowledge." In *Investigations into Assessment in Mathematics Education,* edited by M. Niss, 113–41. Dordrecht, the Netherlands: Kluwer.

BOURBAKI, N. 1999. *Elements of Mathematics*. New York: Springer-Verlag.

COBB, P. 1996. "The Mind or the Culture? A Coordination of Sociocultural and Cognitive Constructivism." In *Constructivism: Theory, Perspectives, and Practice,* edited by C. T. Fosnot, ch. 3. New York: Teachers College Press.

———. 1997. "Instructional Design and Reform: A Plea for Developmental Research in Context." In Beishuizen et al. 1997, 273–89.

DAVIS, P., AND R. HERSH 1981. *The Mathematical Experience*. Boston: Birkhäuser.

DEHN, M. 1983. "The Mentality of the Mathematician: A Characterization." Translated by A. Shenitzer. *The Mathematical Intelligencer* 5(2): 18–26.

DE LANGE, J. 1992. "Critical Factors for Real Changes in Mathematics Learning." In *Assessment and Learning of Mathematics,* edited by G. C. Leder, 305–29. Hawthorn, Victoria: Australian Council for Educational Research.

DESCARTES, R. 1637. *Discours de la méthode pour bien conduire sa raison et chercher la varité dans les sciences plus la diotrique, les meteores, et la geometrie, qui sont des essais de cette methode.* Leyde: I. Maire.

DOLK, M. 1997. *Onmiddellijk onderwijsgedrag over denken en handelen van leraren in onmiddellijke onderwijssituaties.* Utrecht, the Netherlands: W.C.C.

DOWKER, A. 1992. "Computational Estimation Strategies of Professional Mathematicians." *Journal for Research in Mathematics Education* 23(1): 45–55.

DUCKWORTH, E. 1987. *The Having of Wonderful Ideas and Other Essays on Teaching and Learning.* New York: Teachers College Press.

FOSNOT, C. T. 1989. *Enquiring Teachers, Enquiring Learners.* New York: Teachers College Press.

———. 1993. "Learning to Teach, Teaching to Learn: The Center for Constructivist Teaching/Teacher Preparation Project." *Teaching Education* 5(2): 69–78.

———, ed. 1996. *Constructivism: Theory, Perspectives, and Practice.* New York: Teachers College Press.

FOSNOT, C. T., AND M. DOLK. 2001. *Young Mathematicians at Work: Constructing Number Sense, Addition, and Subtraction.* Portsmouth, NH: Heinemann.

FOSNOT, C. T., M. DOLK, M. VAN DEN HEUVEL-PANHUIZEN, B. HILTON, A. WOLF, AND T. N. BAILEY. 2001. Evaluation of the Mathematics in the City Project: Standardized Achievement Test Results. Paper presented at the annual conference of the American Educational Research Association, Seattle, April.

FREUDENTHAL, H. 1968. "Why to Teach Mathematics So As to Be Useful." *Educational Studies in Mathematics* 1: 3–8.

———. 1973. *Mathematics as an Educational Task.* Dordrecht, the Netherlands: Reidel.

———. 1975. "Pupils' Achievements Internationally Compared—the IEA." *Educational Studies in Mathematics* 6: 127–86.

———. 1991. *Revisiting Mathematics Education: The China Lectures.* Dordrecht, the Netherlands: Kluwer.

GAGNÉ, R. 1965. *The Conditions of Learning*. London: Holt, Rinehart, and Winston.

GAUSS, K. F. (1777–1855). 1808. Letter to Bolyai.

GRAVEMEIJER, K. P. E. 1999. "How Emergent Models May Foster the Constitution of Formal Mathematics." *Mathematical Thinking and Learning* 1(2): 155–77.

———. 2000. A Local Instruction Theory on Measuring and Flexible Arithmetic. Paper presented at the International Conference of Mathematics Educators, Tokyo, Japan, August.

GUEDJ, D. 1996. *Numbers: The Universal Language*. Paris: Gallimard. English translation, 1997. New York: Harry Abrams.

HERSH, R. 1997. *What Is Mathematics, Really?* London: Oxford University Press.

JAWORSKI, B. 1995. *Investigating Mathematics Teaching: A Constructivist Enquiry*. London: Falmer.

JEANS, SIR JAMES. QUOTED IN NEWMAN, J. R., ED. 1956. *The World of Mathematics*. New York: Simon and Schuster.

KAMII, C. 1985. *Young Children Reinvent Arithmetic*. New York: Teachers College Press.

———. 1989. *Young Children Continue to Reinvent Arithmetic: Second Grade*. New York: Teachers College Press.

KAMII, C. (WITH S. J. LIVINGSTON). 1993. *Young Children Continue to Reinvent Arithmetic: Third Grade*. New York: Teachers College Press.

KAMII, C., AND A. DOMINICK. 1998. "The Harmful Effects of Algorithms in Grades 1–4." In *The Teaching and Learning of Algorithms in School Mathematics*, edited by L. Morrow and M. Kenney. Reston, VA: National Council of Teachers of Mathematics.

KAMII, C., A. DOMINICK, AND G. DECLARK. 1997. "Teaching to Facilitate 'Progressive Schematization' or Reflective Abstraction?" *The Constructivist* 12(1): 9–14.

KARLIN, S. 1983. Eleventh R. A. Fisher Memorial Lecture. Royal Society, 20 April.

KEREKES, J., AND C. T. FOSNOT. 1998. "Using Pictures with Constraints to Develop Multiplication Strategies." *The Constructivist* 13(2): 15–20.

KORTHAGEN, F., AND J. KESSEL. 1999. "Linking Theory and Practice: Changing the Pedagogy of Teacher Education." *Educational Researcher* 28(4): 4–17.

LEIBNIZ, G. W. (1646–1716). Quoted in Simmons, G. 1992. *Calculus Gems*. New York: McGraw Hill.

LORENZ, J. H. 1997. "Is Mental Calculation Just Strolling Around in an Imaginary Number Space?" In Beishuizen et al. 1997, 199–213.

MA, L. 1999. *Knowing and Teaching Elementary Mathematics*. Mahwah, NJ: Erlbaum.

McDuff, D. 1991. *Mathematical Notices* 38(3): 185–87.

Mittag-Leffler, G. Quoted in Rose, N. 1988. *Mathematical Maxims and Minims.* Raleigh, NC: Rome.

National Council for Teachers of Mathematics. 1989. *Curriculum and Evaluation Standards for School Mathematics.* Reston, VA: NCTM.

———. 2000. *Principles and Standards for School Mathematics.* Reston, VA: NCTM.

Pascal, B. 1670. *Pensées de Pascal sur la religion et sur quelques autres subjets.* Paris: Garnier.

Piaget, J. 1965. *The Child's Conception of Number.* New York: Routledge.

———. 1970. *Structuralism.* New York: Harper & Row.

———. 1977. *The Development of Thought: Equilibration of Cognitive Structures.* New York: Viking.

Plato (ca. 429–347 b.c.). Quoted in Newman, J. R., ed. 1956. *The World of Mathematics.* New York: Simon and Schuster.

Poisson, S. Quoted in *Mathematics Magazine* 64(1), 1991.

Schifter, D., and C. T. Fosnot. 1993. *Reconstructing Mathematics Education: Stories of Teachers Meeting the Challenge of Reform.* New York: Teachers College Press.

Simon, M. 1995. "Reconstructing Mathematics Pedagogy from a Constructivist Perspective." *Journal for Research in Mathematics Education* 26: 114–45.

Shaw, J. B. Quoted in Rose, N. 1988. *Mathematical Maxims and Minims,* Raleigh, NC: Rome.

Steffe, L., E. Glasersfeld, J. Richards, and P. Cobb. 1983. *Children's Counting Types.* New York: Praeger.

Streefland, L. 1981. "Cito's kommagetallen leerdoelgericht getoestst" ["Cito's Decimals Tested in a Criterion-Referenced Way"]. Willem Bartjens, 1(1): 34–44.

———. 1985. "Mathematics as an Activity and Reality as a Source." *Nieuwe Wiskrant* 5(1): 60–67.

Treffers, A. 1987. *Three Dimensions: A Model of Goal and Theory Description in Mathematics Instruction.* The Wiskobas Project. Dordrecht, the Netherlands: Reidel.

———. 1991. "Realistic Mathematics Education in the Netherlands 1980–1990. In *Realistic Mathematics Education in Primary School,* edited by L. Streefland, Series on Research in Education, no. 9 (CD-ß Press). Utrecht, the Netherlands: Utrecht University.

van den Heuvel-Panhuizen, M. 1996. *Assessment and Realistic Mathematic Education.* Series on Research in Education, no. 19 (CD-ß Press). Utrecht, the Netherlands: Utrecht University.

————. 2000. Student Achievement in Mathematics in the City Viewed Through a Microscopic Lens. Paper presented at the International Conference of Mathematics Educators, Tokyo, Japan, August.

VAN DEN HEUVEL PANHUIZEN, M., C. T. FOSNOT, AND M. DOLK. 1999. Internal Document, Mathematics in the City Assessment Instrument.

VAN GALEN, F., M. DOLK, E. FEIJS, V. JONKER, N. RUESINK, AND W. UITTENBOGAARD. 1991. *Interactieve video in de nascholing rekenen-wiskunde.* [Interactive Video for Inservice in Mathematics Education] Utrecht, the Netherlands: Universiteit Utrecht CD-ß press.

WOODARD, M. 2000. Mathematical Quotation Server: http://math.furman .edu/~mwoodard/mqs/mquot.shtml

ZOLKOWER, B. 1998. "Bridging the Gap Between School Mathematics and Common Sense: A Realistic Turn." *The Constructivist* 13(2): 5–14.

ZOLKOWER, B., M. DOLK, AND C. T. FOSNOT. Beyond Word and Story Problems: On the Use of Picture-Based Contexts for Mathematizing. Unpublished document.

INDEX

Tb/1.50